YOU'RE HERE FOR A REASON

YOU'RE HERE FOR A REASON

The practical and spiritual guide to align with your purpose and awaken your career

Rebecca Kirk

BANNISTER
PUBLICATIONS

First published in Great Britain in 2023 by

Bannister Publications Ltd, Office 2A Market Hall,
Market Place, Chesterfield, Derbyshire. S40 1ARG.

ISBN 978-1-909813-99-1

Typeset by Bannister Publications Ltd.

This book was self-published by Bannister Publications.
For more information on self-publishing visit:
www.bannisterpublications.com

Printed and bound in Great Britain by Short Run Press Ltd, Exeter, Devon.

MIX
Paper from
responsible sources
FSC
www.fsc.org   FSC® C014540

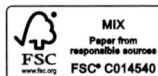

Dedication

For my family whose belief in me has helped me emerge
from my chrysalis and open my wings.

And for the Universe for awakening me to my calling
and affording me the means with which to pursue it.

Book Resources

To access the free extra resources that accompany this book go to:

rebeccakirk.co.uk/book-resources

Contents

*You're here for
a reason.
I truly believe that.*

REBECCA KIRK

Introduction

I believe that we are all here for a reason, whether or not we know what that is or are living it out yet. Having a reason for being is one of the most profound needs we have as humans. The quest for meaning and purpose has always been part of our evolutionary journey. And the events surrounding the pandemic, in 2020 and 2021, have only served to exacerbate this need for many. As a spiritual career coach, I have witnessed more and more people lose connection with their work and their true identity and question the very core of their existence.

The planet is undergoing a major shift, a shake up of sorts. Many of us are being forced to re-evaluate what is truly important to us. If we can take anything from these past few years, it is to recognise the power that a challenge can have to act as a catalyst. A catalyst which can wake us up from our slumber and stop us from staying stuck in a situation which no longer serves us. You might have witnessed this through a friend or colleague who was made redundant from a job they hated but were too afraid to resign from and then it turned out to be the best thing that could have happened to them.

This shift has led me to create a quantum leap in my coaching business. I could no longer coach people in their career without bringing spirituality into the mix. I see the two as intrinsically linked and mutually supportive. The challenges you face in your career can force you to open up to your spirituality. To look for new support tools and a deeper connection to help anchor yourself through the choppy waters. And similarly, your spirituality can support you through your career challenge.

It is no longer enough to simply update your CV and do a bit of networking if you're wanting to feel truly fulfilled in your job. Creating a profound and sustainable change must go deeper. It must look at your ways of thinking, your belief system, your whole being.

It is time for us all to awaken. To live more intentionally and become fully conscious of our desires, as well as our patterns, our limiting thoughts and our fears. To bring out into the open the things which have long been buried and squashed down. To live our lives with greater freedom and authenticity. To give ourselves permission to enjoy the fruits of our labours. To empower ourselves to create working lives filled with peace, purpose and prosperity instead of seeing ourselves as victims, playing small or just accepting our circumstances.

What this book is about

This book is about purpose and how to align with it. It is a practical and spiritual guidebook for the journey through a career crossroads onto a path of greater fulfilment. It centres around a tried-and-tested coaching process which I have created and refined over many years and use with my one-to-one clients.

This book offers a fresh approach to finding purpose which enables you to awaken through your career challenge and enjoy more happiness in your working life. It looks at the *foundations* of making a successful change in your career, not just the outer aspects. It helps you to make a *conscious* choice whether to stay in your current job or to pivot into something completely different which brings you more fulfilment.

So many people are searching for purpose. In my work as a spiritual career coach, this has been very evident to me. Over the past three years, sixty five percent of my clients, when beginning their work with me, declared that they did not feel connected to the reason why they did their job. The vast majority of those clients also stated that this lack of connection had negatively impacted their wellbeing and their relationships, often leading to stress and depression.

Conversely, as multiple studies have shown, a clear sense of purpose can lead to physical and mental health improvements and often to a longer life. The Japanese concept of 'Ikigai' (which translates as 'reason for being') has long been considered an important philosophy for living a more fulfilling and healthy life.

This book and the process I am about to share with you is less about 'finding' your purpose and more about 'aligning' with your purpose. 'Finding' implies that your purpose lies somewhere on the outside. 'Aligning', however, implies that your purpose is already within you and that it's more about bringing your outer circumstances into resonance with who you already are deep inside (but have perhaps forgotten or disconnected from).

Aligning is firstly about awakening within to your own truth. It's about connecting to your own essence, to your heart and to your soul. And once you've connected within, it's then about consciously bringing your life and career into alignment with that truth and that essence. This book is designed to help you do just that.

My coaching experience and my personal experience, alongside years of extensive reading of spiritual text, has formed the research basis for much of this book. I will be sharing stories from some of my clients, along with a few of my own, which I hope will inspire you and open your mind and your heart to what is truly possible for you.

Stories from clients such as Fiona , who left behind her accounting career to follow her long-held mission to enable people to discover greater wellbeing through dance and movement. And Pratesh who found a way to align with his gifts and passions by setting up a decluttering business.

If you read this book thoroughly, with an open mind and commit to doing the work, you will gain:

- Clarity on what your purpose is.

- Confidence in your own ability within your current job or the confidence to make a career change.

- Belief in yourself and a deeper feeling of self-worth.

- Inspiration to energise and motivate you to make a potential career change.

- Hope in the possibility of having a purposeful career.

Why I wrote this book

When I left my last 'regular' job in the corporate world and reached my career crossroads back in 2010, I navigated my way through without a definitive roadmap. I knew that my life had to change and, after repeating the same patterns for a number of years, I was finally prepared to take the leap of faith needed to create a transformative shift, from which I have never looked back. But I did it the hard way.

This book is a product of my own search for purpose and fulfilment and the spiritual awakening journey I have been on alongside it. I wrote this book to provide you with a shortcut to discover the clarity, belief and motivation you need to move you through your career crossroads and enjoy a life of greater purpose. And to combine all the tools, philosophies and approaches which have supported me in discovering my purpose, into a single book.

I have benefited hugely from the wisdom and learnings shared by a number of wonderful teachers along the way to my own career alignment. However, I also felt like there was a gap for something which combined career and spirituality in a way which really spoke to me. I was looking for something which allowed for my own interpretation of spirituality, and which went down deeper into the foundations of what made me tick at work.

This is a book I have been guided to write. It is a calling and one which I simply could not ignore any longer. I have had this calling for several years now, but there were many lessons I needed to learn and many roads I had to go down first. I needed to awaken more fully, which I did following the passing of my beloved Mum in 2019. This was an act of grace. It led me to doing some intense inner work and gain a new awareness of spirituality which means I have something deeper to share now.

The Universe knew the exact timing of my mission and once I surrendered to that, I relaxed and tapped into the flow of creative energy which is enabling these words to come out onto the page with such lightness and ease. And the same can happen for you. Whether your mission is writing a book, starting your own business or simply showing up to your current job with greater passion or making a bigger impact.

One thing I know with great certainty is that your career challenge, as with any life challenge, can also become a portal into your awakening. For me, the acute need for clarity, for support, for answers along my career journey forced me into deepening my connection to the Universe. And this, in turn, is what has supported me in aligning with my true purpose. It's a beautifully symbiotic relationship.

Ahead of you lies the opportunity to discover and surrender to your calling. And to deepen your spiritual connection in the process. This can be challenging work at times, but it can also be immensely joyful, life-affirming and expansive.

Who this book is for

This book is for people who are searching for greater purpose and fulfilment in their working life and are also on a spiritual path (be that simply spiritually curious, fully awakened, or somewhere in between).

Perhaps you can relate to some of the following:

- Feeling stuck and lost at a career crossroads and not sure which path to take.

- Yearning to do work which feels more meaningful and to make more of a difference in the world.

- Having a sense that there is something else out there you are meant to be doing but can't put your finger on it.

- Contemplating making a career change but not knowing where to start and terrified of taking a risk.

- Searching for an approach which is deeper and more meaningful than what traditional careers advice offers.

- Disappointed that you have not realised anywhere near your potential yet and that time is ticking away.

- Overthinking everything and losing perspective on what's truly important.

- Knowing deep down that simply updating your CV and diving into another job search is not going to cut it for you anymore.

- Having hit a milestone birthday and now asking yourself, "Why am I here?"

- Shuddering when you think about doing the same job for the next 25 years.

- Feeling alone and unsupported on your spiritual path.

Or maybe some of the messages I have received from people seeking help resonate with you:

"I feel like the job I have is misaligned with who I am and what I want to spend my time doing and feel lost."

"I am at a crossroads with my business/work life and have reached burn out. I have low confidence, self-doubt and imposter syndrome which prevents me from being as successful as I could be."

"I've been working in big tech and startups for the past six years, in a role I'm good at and well compensated for, but I truly dislike it and know I'll regret having done this for many more years. I'd like to move from a place of analysis paralysis to real reflection and action and have confidence in what the path to my next career looks like."

"I have felt increasingly unconfident and unsatisfied in my job, and I want to explore what direction to go in. I have contradictory thoughts about what I think I want and would love for someone to help me unpick and make sense of it all. I'm desperate to find my spark, what lights me up, finding a purpose but am struggling to find direction."

"I am on sabbatical from my corporate job, I am looking to find my inner purpose and find fulfilment. Having tried a number of paths which haven't worked, I feel a bit lost at this moment."

I wrote this book for all of you.

This book can be a valuable resource for you in any career circumstance, whether you are currently employed, self-employed or unemployed following redundancy, having lost your job or having taken time out to raise children or go on a career break. And this book is also relevant to people from a whole range of career backgrounds, just as my methods have been within my one-to-one coaching practice. The ideas equally apply whether you are a teacher, a lawyer, a marketeer, or an artist.

What my readers do have in common (as with my clients) alongside the search for purpose is their openness to a more holistic and spiritual approach. They are people who are willing to go beyond their pure physical existence and explore their deeper identity and a higher consciousness as part of their career change journey.

This book does not focus on (nor exclude) any particular religion but incorporates a secular approach to spirituality. Whilst I use the term 'Universe' in reference to that higher being, I invite you to use whatever language resonates with you – which might be God, Source, the Divine, Consciousness or something else entirely.

The spiritual dimension to this book means that we will be exploring concepts such as Divine Timing, callings, the Higher Self and intuition. We will bring practices such as meditation, prayer and visualisation into the mix. And we will acknowledge the power of your vibration throughout. But we will be doing this in conjunction with the practical and grounded topics which are equally important such as transferable skills, values and goal setting.

How to use this book

This book has been written in a way which takes you on a journey – I call it your Career Alignment Journey.

This journey is divided into four parts:

PART 1: PREPARING THE WAY

To make a profound and sustainable transformation in your career, it is important that you approach this journey from a place of grounded stability rather than from a place of heightened emotion or chaos. In Part 1 we will discover some practices and concepts to enable you to feel calm and connected and to create the mental, physical and energetic space with which to welcome in your purpose.

PART 2: AWAKENING YOUR TRIPLE PURPOSE

We get to the heart of the matter in Part 2 as we open up to the topic of purpose. Here I will share with you what I call your *Triple Purpose* which comprises of your Higher Purpose, your Life Purpose and your Career Purpose. We will look at the inter-connectedness of those three and how a broader definition of purpose can support you both in your work and in your life.

PART 3: PLANTING YOUR ROOTS

In Part 3, we journey into the depths of your Being to help you make sense of who you truly are and to give you the firm foundation with which to align your career. The central theme at the heart of this book is the Purpose Tree. Each chapter in this part focuses on one of the four different 'roots' of the tree from which your Career Purpose will emerge. This also gives you the opportunity to reconnect to any parts of yourself you have perhaps lost connection with over time.

PART 4: ALIGNING YOUR CAREER

Finally in Part 4, we move into the action phase of the journey. We begin drawing together everything from the previous three parts so you can get clear on what it is you want and create a plan which brings focus and direction to your onward journey. We will also look at taking active steps on aligning with your purpose and creating some real momentum for change.

Each part builds on the previous one. Whilst it has been written in a linear way, I also invite you to listen to any intuitive feelings around which part or chapter you are most called to read at any point. For example, if you sense you have a lot of resistance or stuck energy, you may choose to go to Chapter 4 (Letting go of Resistance) sooner. For some people, it works better to meet this resistance head on. For others, the resistance emerges as they progress through the process. Listen within as to what the best approach is for you.

I also want to point out that each part has its own energy vibration which I recommend you become aware of and consciously tune into. The energy of Part 1 where you are focused on your inner state may well feel very different to the energy of Part 4 where you are moving into action. It can be helpful to acknowledge this rather than wondering if something is wrong. And to create a container of time or a ritual to support you in opening the space for each part.

Each chapter has some practical ideas or coaching exercises for you to use. To get the best results from this book, it is vital that you roll your sleeves up and do the work. Set some quality time aside to engage in the suggested activities. Where there are a number of suggestions, again I encourage you to listen within as to what you feel most drawn towards doing.

One thing which has been a big game-changer for me personally, and for so many of my clients, is having a Daily Spiritual Practice. Throughout this book there will be ideas which can form part of your practice. Equally, feel free to bring your own practice into this journey.

Aligning with your purpose can take time. It is absolutely possible that whilst reading this book you may have a sudden breakthrough or a lightbulb moment which changes everything overnight. However, it is also important to see this as a journey and a 'moving towards' your purpose over time. My advice to you is not to rush it. Take your time with it. Dive into this journey. Invest yourself in the process. That is what will bring you the most lasting transformation. And it will make the journey a whole lot more enjoyable. Take it slowly and let everything from each chapter sink in before rushing onto the next.

There may be chapters in this book which you find easy and enjoyable, whilst others you find challenging or triggering. This is normal. I encourage you to stick with it through the pages which trigger you and open up to where this work needs to go for you. To acknowledge the parts of you that perhaps need to heal.

I also encourage you to be open to the different possibilities which may emerge from reading this book. And to let go of any specific expectations you may have around the outcome. Sometimes, clients come to me expecting to leave their current job through the coaching process but instead end up discovering a deeper connection to it. As a result of reading this book you may be called to begin your own healing journey, which then leads you on to awakening to your purpose. Trust that you have found this book at exactly the right time and that your journey will unfold in its own perfect way.

There are certain points, ideas and concepts which you may notice being repeated throughout the book. This has been done consciously to emphasise some of the most important things I want to land with you.

And one final note about the language I use. If you are not in a job at present, whenever I talk about your 'current career' then please substitute this for your *most recent* career.

Resources

To accompany this book, there is a range of free resources available to support you on your journey and take your learnings to the next level.

This includes PDF worksheets for all of the key topics such as your Values, your Purpose Tree and your Career Alignment Plan which you can either print off or complete online. Using the worksheets will help you structure your thoughts, gain further clarity and also provide you with reminders of the insights you generate.

Access and download your free Book Resources now at: rebeccakirk.co.uk/book-resources

Journalling

I want to give a special nod to journalling right from the outset as a powerful accompaniment to this book. Journalling is the therapeutic practice of writing down your thoughts, feelings, insights and intuitive nudges. Almost inevitably this book will stir up some things for you and it is important that you let everything have room to breathe. Often, seeing things in black and white instead of letting them just swim around in your head can make a huge difference.

I invite you to use a journal to capture things such as:

- Thoughts or ideas around potential new career paths.

- Fears or limiting thought patterns which are keeping you stuck.

- Your mood and your energy.

In many of the chapters, I offer you some journalling questions. Answering these questions will create a deeper understanding of the concepts and ideas presented. Through this self-enquiry, you are more likely to have some 'a-ha' moments and generate fresh insights around your current situation.

I recommend that you buy a new journal to symbolise a fresh start and to keep it by your side as you work your way through the chapters.

My deepest wish

I am so happy to have you here and that you have this book in your hands or on your screen. This in itself is a powerful step towards awakening your purpose. You are signalling to the Universe that you are ready and open to change.

My deepest wish is that this book leads you down the path towards enjoying a fully lived life of purpose just as I have been blessed to enjoy. And that it provides a catalyst to your own awakening, wherever you are on your spiritual path.

If you are ready to take a quantum leap in your working life, then it's time to look at things from a new angle. Open your mind and your heart and get ready to align with your purpose!

Sending you love and light for your journey,

Rebecca x

PART 1:
PREPARING THE WAY

*What's for you
won't go by you.*

SCOTTISH PROVERB

CHAPTER 1:
Trusting your Path

We begin the journey by exploring the power of trust and the impact that it can have on your inner state of being and, consequently, your ability to be a vessel for positive change.

Trusting your path means opening up to the timings of the Universe instead of trying to force things to happen on your own watch. It means enjoying the journey that you are on and seeing any challenges as opportunities for growth. And it means avoiding the pitfalls of making reactive decisions which are not founded in a deep connection to who you truly are and what is for your highest good.

However uncomfortable, frustrating or challenging your current career situation is, what would it feel like to know that, right now, you are right where you are meant to be? How would if feel to fully accept all that has happened and to embrace your own story? What would change for you if you were able to let go of comparing your path to that of others or grasping for answers about your purpose?

When clients come to me wanting to find their purpose, it is often accompanied by, at the very least, a sense of urgency and, in some cases, a very palpable sense of desperation. I get it. Doing a job without true meaning or purpose can really weigh heavy. And, over time, it can make you feel desperate for solutions. It can make you feel like time is running out. That if you don't find an answer soon to one of your life's biggest questions, then you're somehow going to miss the boat. It may also mean continuing to experience the often excruciating discomfort of being in a situation in which you feel lost, miserable and possibly even ill.

However, making a knee-jerk decision from a heightened emotional state to try and solve a career crossroads conundrum rarely brings about a profound or lasting change. Nothing is to be gained from quitting your current job in a state of despondency and despair, only to jump straight into a similar role, hoping it will be more aligned this time around.

If you feel like you are on the verge of making such a decision or perhaps you have a strong sense of urgency which is starting to cloud your judgement, I invite you to take a moment now to simply pause and breathe. Try and relax into this journey that you're about to embark on. Open to your spiritual side and your potential to tap into new-found feelings of trust, patience and acceptance. Feelings which will serve your highest good in the long run.

Perhaps this may seem counter-intuitive to what you have been taught, but what is the alternative? What patterns have you perhaps already repeated? Ask yourself, is it time for a step-change and to revolutionise your way of approaching your career challenge and your search for purpose? And if not now, then when?

All of this is not to say that you have to go on suffering through your current circumstances and feelings until you've 'figured everything out'. Throughout this book, I will be suggesting practices and tools which will also enable you to make more immediate changes in your current job or situation that will lead you to feeling calmer and more at peace whilst you work towards career alignment.

Honouring the non-linear path

I have an old university friend who, at the age of 22, knew exactly what she wanted to do straight after completing her degree in criminology back in 1995. She followed her calling to enter the police and has never looked back, rising to the rank of deputy chief constable. I admire her hugely for her single-minded focus and for what she has achieved in following her calling to serve.

From the conversations I have with people, both as a spiritual career coach and outside of my work, this linear career path and single-minded focus is actually quite uncommon. Although, many people assume that everyone else is on a straight trajectory and that if they aren't too then something is wrong with them.

This comparison can trigger much resistance towards the idea of making a career change. Limiting beliefs can surface, such as "I'm too old for a career change" or "I need to just stick with this career I'm in now, I've made my bed so I'd better lie in it." Instead, I encourage you to see your Career Alignment Journey as your own unique path of exploration. And, in that way, you can watch yourself grow and evolve through the choices you make and the callings you feel drawn towards pursuing.

I began my working life in a very different field to the one I'm in now. I was a retail buyer, very much immersed in the commercial, profit-making world. I cannot imagine being in that world now. But I couldn't possibly have known then what I know now (or when I pivoted into coaching back in 2016). I believe that I was meant to go through the challenges and experiences to bring me to where

I am today. I had to get out of alignment so I could feel the deep intense yearning which eventually brought me into alignment. There was certainly no linear path for me! And, in many ways, perhaps my work now tastes all the sweeter for it.

When you're on a spiritual path, you recognise that everything has a reason for existing. You see the growth potential in difficult or challenging situations. Or when things don't quite pan out as you had hoped.

One thing the Ego Self loves to do is to compare itself to others. I really urge you to call on your Higher Self instead, to see the bigger picture and to have faith and trust in your path. (We will explore both the Higher Self and Ego Self later in the book.)

Acceptance

The act of acceptance creates an immediate shift in your vibration. You don't have to *like* your current circumstances, but when you learn to *accept* them, you stop resisting and you surrender. And when you do that, you free up energy and head space for your journey towards a life with greater purpose.

Whatever has already happened in the past does not dictate what lies ahead of you (unless you allow it to). However, your state of being (the extent to which you are able to reside peacefully within your body, mind and spirit) *does* affect what happens in your future. And so, if you are laden down by your past choices, your supposed 'failures', your perceived limitations, your past traumas or your current circumstances, I encourage you now to shake them all off. You are going to learn some new ways of thinking and being which will enable you to embrace a whole new set of circumstances and a whole new level of 'success' (whatever that means to you).

However, I do also want to highlight that what has gone before you could also provide a useful pointer towards discovering what your purpose is. As an example of that, a few years ago I had a client who had just extricated herself from a domestic abuse situation. This intensely challenging life event proved a powerful motivation for her to pursue her dream of becoming a life coach, supporting other women in finding their voices and empowering them to turn their own situations around. It also enabled her to create a stronger connection with her audience, by sharing her personal story and how she managed to successfully navigate a path towards her purpose. As this example illustrates, nothing that happens to us needs ever be wasted. If we choose, we can transmute our challenges into gold.

Divine Timing

Divine Timing is the idea that the Universe has its own schedule for you and that everything is unfolding at exactly the right time, for your highest good. Often, this timing doesn't make a lot of sense. But that's only because you don't have all the information or the bigger picture view that the Universe has. Perhaps you are trying to figure things out purely on the level of the mind. The Universe has the helicopter view on your life and is able to orchestrate things in such a way that is beyond most people's comprehension.

Every single one of us is on our own unique path. Every soul is on its own individual journey through this lifetime. I wish I could give you 100 percent assurance that at the end of reading this book, you will know exactly what your purpose is and that you will immediately be taking the next step. Be that handing your notice in on your current job, applying for a new job, setting a new business up or perhaps embarking on a new qualification.

Whilst that is all entirely possible, my guarantee of an outcome would overlook the fact that there is a higher force at work here that knows exactly what the right timing is for *you*, for *your* highest good. It may be that at the end of this book, you are simply ready to *open up to the possibility* of connecting to your purpose. That is still a significant and very necessary part of the journey. Particularly if you have never truly been open to it before or if you have had some significant blocks to being open to it which have been there for a number of years.

There is a reason why things happen *when* they do and, conversely, when they *don't* happen on your schedule. This can be hugely frustrating and even baffling at times, even for the most spiritually awakened person. Keep in mind that this state of frustration can have a detrimental effect on your vibration and hence your search for purpose, something we will look at more closely in Chapter 2.

I have clients who come to me after having applied for several new jobs they are often highly qualified for, wondering why they keep getting interviews and great feedback only to keep getting turned down at the final stage. My response to their despondency and confusion is always the same. I ask them to consider what the Universe might be trying to communicate to them. How this might be Divine Timing in action. In a scenario like this, the Universe is often protecting them from something which is not for their highest good, whilst the groundwork is being prepared for something in much closer alignment to their purpose.

When I first attempted to write a book back in 2018, I thought I had everything ready. The inspiration was there, and it just 'felt' right. A Hay House writers' workshop and competition was serendipitously put in my path which I thought must have been a sign. I duly attended and completed and submitted my book proposal. It turned out it wasn't the right time. Although I was disappointed not to win, I also remembered that the Universe had other plans for me.

When I look back now, I can see clearly how I wasn't fully ready to receive the messages I needed to communicate. I had a lot of inner spiritual work to do and lots of other career lessons to learn first. I can see how I was meant to have a deeper experience of consciousness and realign my coaching business before I shared my writing with the world. I am truly grateful to the Universe now for holding me back. I could not have written this book without Divine Timing playing a hand in it.

I do also want to highlight that trusting in Diving Timing does not mean that you now simply sit back and wait for the Universe to do its thing whilst you do nothing. Rather than entering into a passive state, your part in this is to stay tuned in to the signs and guidance offered to you and to create an active state of conscious positive thought and energy which helps you maintain faith and a high vibration. And then to take appropriate action as and when the time comes.

Non-attachment and non-grasping

I first came to properly understand the profound wisdom of the Buddhist concept of 'non-attachment' shortly after I launched my first online coaching course a few years ago. I was starting to feel very despondent and unsettled because it wasn't delivering the results I had hoped for after all the hard work I had put into creating it. It was putting me into a state of unease and led me to question myself and my path. Then I realised something. I had totally attached myself and my happiness to the success of the course and was suffering because of that attachment. It was a lesson in non-attachment (thank you, Universe).

Similarly, it is easy to become attached to finding your purpose and the desire for getting clarity on what it is that you're meant to be doing. Attachment can often be accompanied by a feeling of incompleteness before you find or obtain the thing you are attached to. As we shall discover in Chapter 8 when we explore *Your Higher Self*, you are already complete, worthy and whole. What you do for a living is undoubtedly important, but it is not who you truly are. Viewing things in this way and releasing attachment can actually empower your search for purpose and enable you to feel much calmer and happier along the way.

Closely related to the concept of non-attachment is the concept of 'non-grasping'. In his book *A Monk's Guide to Happiness*, former Buddhist monk Gelong Thubten describes grasping as 'our tendency to grab at things in the world around us'. When we grasp, again we put our focus on external things as our source of happiness but, ironically, this often only serves to provide us with a source of stress. The intense *desire* for change or for a certain outcome can become its nemesis.

Often, by the time a client reaches out to me, they have already spent a significant amount of time and energy 'grasping' at ideas, potential career avenues or the promise of a silver bullet from various different sources and simply can't take it anymore.

Here are some of the ways I witness grasping and attachment taking hold in my clients:

- Constantly searching for or applying for new jobs.

- Asking lots of other people for their opinions on what they 'should' be doing.

- Chasing a myriad of thoughts and ideas about a possible new career path.

- Putting their life on hold until they have found their purpose.

- Pinning all their hopes for happiness onto their career.

- Holding on tightly to an aspect of their current job, such as the salary or the status.

- Wondering what they will do or who they will become if they don't find their purpose.

If you can relate to any of this, I invite you now to consider the impact this might be having on your mental and physical state, your vibration and, ultimately, your ability to discover your purpose. What emotions does this type of grasping or attaching bring out in you? How helpful are those emotions to you as you search for the clarity and confidence needed to make an impactful career change?

If you are grasping or attaching at the moment, there is an alternative which we will now take a look at.

Practices for trusting your path

Here are some suggested practices for you to try, which can help you let go of attaching and grasping and begin to trust your path more.

1. Observe your thoughts and feelings

- Begin by identifying the thoughts you are having about your next career move or those which underly any actions you might currently be taking, such as searching for new jobs.

- Do you suspect that those thoughts come from a place of trust or from a place of fear? Is there a sense of flow and ease behind them? Or do you suspect you might be chasing or hustling in some way?

- Now tune in to the feelings and the energy in your body when you think about your career path and any changes you are trying to make.

- Is that energy light and spacious? Or does it feel heavy or burdened, perhaps with a knot in your stomach? Your body will always give you the clues you need.

- Once you have observed any thoughts and feelings stemming from attachment and grasping, you then have a *choice* to instead call in trust.

2. Visualise letting go

- Close your eyes and take a few deep breaths to connect within.

- Set your intention around what you want to create, achieve or experience (you could start out with something smaller and more immediate than finding your purpose).

- Imagine putting that intention and all that you hope it will bring you into a balloon. Fill the balloon with your deepest wishes and any associated positive emotions.

- Tie the balloon with a piece of coloured string (whatever colour you feel drawn to).

- Visualise the details on your hand as you loosen your grip on the string and then let the string go and the balloon be taken by the wind.

- Picture yourself watching the balloon drift off out into the Universe where it will be received with love and support.

- As it soars into the sky, trust that Divine Timing is at work and that the Universe will support you with your intention in a way which is for your highest good.

3. Call on your Higher Self

- When you grasp or attach yourself to a particular outcome or thing, recognise this as simply the fear-based Ego Self at work.

- Instead of being taken over by the Ego Self, let this signal the need for you to call on your Higher Self. (Once you become aware, the Ego Self naturally loses its grip).

- The Higher Self is that part of you which knows that things are all happening for your highest good and on Divine Timing's schedule.

- You can practice connecting with your Higher Self through, for example, meditation and prayer (we will look at this in more detail in Chapter 8).

- The main thing for now is to simply recognise the Ego Self at work and to know that you have an alternative to call on.

4. Be more present

- When you learn to become truly present in each moment, you stop ruminating on your past or worrying about the future. This is where your true power lies and your connection to spirit, and its guidance, can be accessed.

- If you find yourself getting caught up in anxious thoughts about how your path is going to unfold, gently and lovingly bring yourself back to the present moment.

- Similarly, if you are stuck on some aspect of your past and certain choices you have made and any beliefs about what is therefore possible for you, refocus into the now.

- An easy way to connect with the present moment is to become aware of your breath and your surroundings, using your senses. This can break the cycle of repetitive thought and rumination in an instant.

5. Ask the Universe for help

- Another simple way to practice trusting your path is to communicate with the Universe.

- Ask for support, particularly with any aspects of trusting your path or letting go of attachment and grasping that you may be finding more challenging, such as accepting your past or understanding why things aren't very clear to you right now.

- Write out a prayer to the Universe and then say it out loud.

- After you have said your prayer, listen out for the guidance, the signs or the intuitive nudges which will be given to you over the following days and weeks.

Here is a prayer I would like to offer you to get started:

Dear Universe,

Help me open up to trusting more in your timing than my own.

Grant me the unwavering faith which allows me to know without question that you have a higher plan for me which far surpasses anything that I can conceive of with my human mind.

Allow me to enjoy this journey I am on and to see all that has gone before me as an important part of my evolution rather than something which I have failed at.

I now choose to listen out for your guidance as I surrender to your higher plan for me. And trust that the right people and the right circumstances will show up for me at the right time so that I may move towards living in alignment with my true purpose.

I relax and rejoice as I trust in my path now.

CHAPTER HIGHLIGHTS

- Trusting your path means opening up to the timings of the Universe, enjoying the journey and avoiding the pitfalls of making reactive decisions.

- What lies ahead on your career path is determined by your state of being more than your current or past circumstances.

- A non-linear career path offers great potential for growth and evolution.

- Divine Timing is the idea that the Universe has its own schedule for you and that everything is unfolding at exactly the right time, for your highest good.

- Acceptance of your current situation creates a shift in your vibration and frees up energy and head space for your journey towards purpose.

Journalling questions

What are your feelings towards your own path and your current circumstances? What is your overriding emotional state? Try not to judge anything which arises for you.

How much do your past or current circumstances influence your belief in what's possible for you in the future?

What are you hoping for which has perhaps led you to reading this book, such as a fulfilling new career?

In what ways might you be 'attached' to that happening for you? In what ways might you be 'grasping' for what you want right now?

Which of the practices to help you trust your path are you willing to have a go at in the next seven days?

Everything is energy and that's all there is to it. Match the frequency of the reality you want and you cannot help but get that reality. It can be no other way.

ALBERT EINSTEIN

CHAPTER 2:
Upgrading your Energy

Raising your spiritual energy and vibration is another way that you can prepare yourself to discover and align with your purpose. If you've started incorporating some of the suggested practices already, you will hopefully be noticing at least a subtle shift in your energy. By bringing more awareness to this energy and discovering some ways to raise your vibration, you can become an attracting force for the life of purpose which you long for (and have a lot more fun along the way).

Everything is energy

Everything in the Universe is made up of energy which vibrates. From the cells of your body right through to the clothes that you wear and the chair you are currently sat on. This is one thing which the world of science and spirituality *can* agree on. We are all vibrational beings. We all emit a vibrational frequency which can be felt by others. This may also be described as your 'aura', your 'energy field' or giving off 'vibes'.

You can sense the vibration or energy of another person when you meet them or when you walk into a room. Whether it's a positive, light and uplifting energy which draws you in or a heavy, negative energy which repels you. Sometimes you may not even realise that you are being affected by someone's energy, and vice versa.

What impacts your energy

There are many things which impact your energy. It can be very empowering to become aware of these things, as it means that you aren't then at the mercy of them. With awareness, you can make some conscious choices to 'manage' your energy and create a higher vibration.

Your energy is impacted by:

- Your thoughts
- Your words
- Your beliefs
- Your emotions
- Your actions
- Your environment
- Smells and aromas
- Other people (their energy, their words, their beliefs)
- The food and drink you consume
- The music you listen to
- The TV programmes you watch

I encourage you to start noticing more how these different things impact *your* energy.

Your energy is always attracting

One of the main reasons why I encourage you to become aware of and consciously raise your energy vibration is because of the impact it can have on your ability to attract and manifest what you want. Plus, as a huge side benefit, when you live in a higher vibration state, life will feel more peaceful and enjoyable.

You are *always* attracting, whatever your vibrational frequency. However, the thing to be mindful of is that in a high vibration state you will be attracting what you *do* want (through positive alignment) and in a low vibration state you will be attracting what you *don't* want (through negative alignment).

The chart on the next page Illustrates this point using a scale of frequencies linked to various different emotions. This is adapted from the *The Map of Consciousness*[2] by Dr David Hawkins, a scale created using a unique muscle-testing method from over 20 years of research. The emotions of love, joy, peace and enlightenment were measured as emitting the highest frequencies, whilst emotions such as fear, guilt and shame were seen to emit some of the lowest frequencies.

To further understand this point, it can also be helpful to imagine yourself as a transmission tower standing high up on a hill. The images you see on your screen or the station you tune into, that is, the things which show up in your life, reflect the frequency you are emitting. When you turn the TV or radio on, you have to tune into a certain frequency in order to watch or listen to the programme you want to watch or listen to. And so it is with your life. You must get onto the same frequency of that which you *want*.

HIGH FREQUENCY   **ATTRACTION**

Enlightenment	700-1000
Peace	600
Joy	540
Love	500
Reason	400
Acceptance	350
Willingness	310
Neutrality	250
Courage	200
Pride	175
Anger	150
Desire	125
Fear	100
Grief	75
Apathy	50
Guilt	30
Shame	20

Positive Alignment

**ATTRACTING
WHAT YOU
DO WANT**

Negative Alignment

**ATTRACTING
WHAT YOU
DON'T WANT**

LOW FREQUENCY   **ATTRACTION**

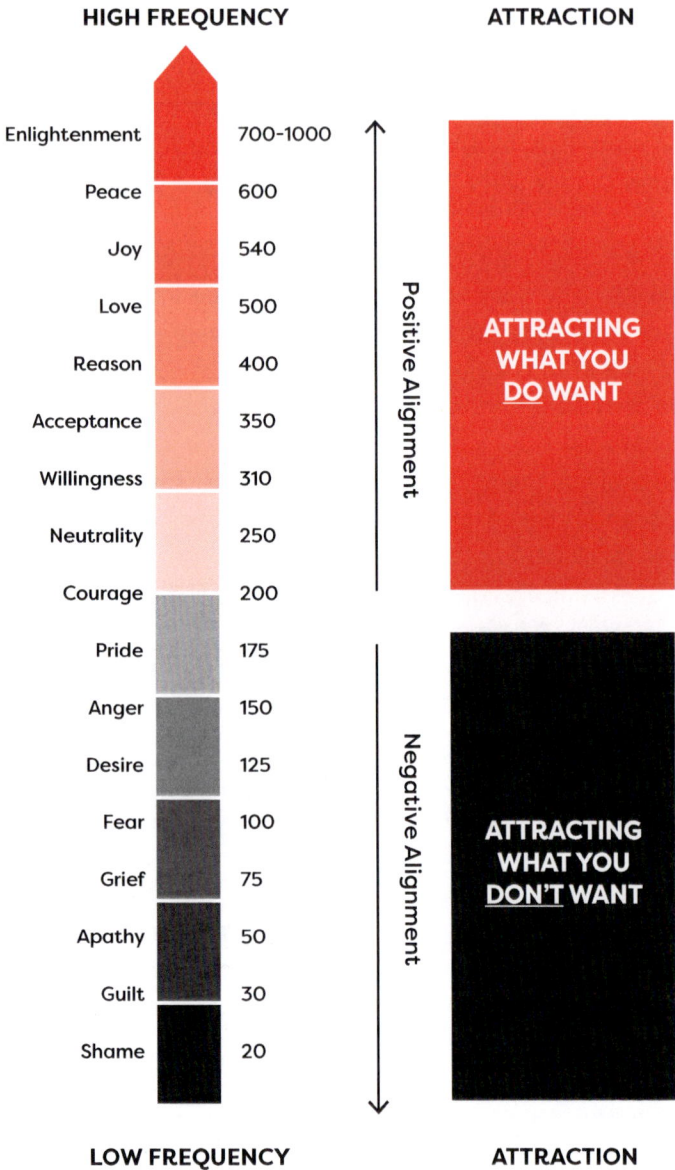

(Adapted from *The Map of Consciousness* by Dr David Hawkins)

How your energy could be impacting your search for purpose

When you consider your current situation and how you feel about your career, what is your predominant emotion? For instance, do you feel joyful, accepting or courageous? Or are you more towards the lower end of the scale of feeling fearful, guilty or angry in some way?

Some common examples of how lower vibration emotions can emerge whilst at a career crossroads include:

- Feeling guilty about focusing on your own happiness.

- Feeling angry or resentful towards an employer for how you have been treated.

- Being fearful about what the future holds.

- Feeling worried about letting go of your current job.

- Feeling a sense of loss or grief from a career, job or project which didn't work out.

- Experiencing shame around losing your job (or another life or career event).

- Worrying about what other people will think of you if you make a career change.

Do any of these resonate with you? I strongly urge you to recognise if and where you might be emitting a low vibration frequency and make a conscious decision to turn it around. The cost of not doing so could mean that you will continue to attract what you *don't* want, such as:

- Staying stuck in a job you hate.

- Feeling lost and confused at your crossroads.

- Having a stressful working life which is leading you towards burnout.

- Repeating the same pattern of being undervalued by your employer.

- Continuing to live an unfulfilled life where you are limiting your potential.

How upgrading your energy will support you

Conversely, if you choose to upgrade your energy and operate from a higher vibration state, your search for purpose will become much easier. Through your energy, you will be empowering yourself to attract:

- The right people who can guide and support you on your path.

- The right circumstances for your new path to unfold.

- The right employer/clients when the time comes for you to put yourself out there.

- The abundance you are yearning for, be that money, time, love or peace.

- The wellbeing and balance which will make this journey sustainable.

Whilst you may not yet have clarity on your purpose, I encourage you to prepare the way by becoming more conscious of your energy and to welcome in some new methods to move you into a higher vibrational state (however small to begin with).

Ten ways to upgrade your energy

Here are some suggested ways that you can upgrade your energy. See which ones resonate with you.

1. Focus more on what you <u>do</u> want

Firstly, recognise that your thoughts hold a vibration. Catch yourself as soon as you begin getting lost in any negative thoughts about your current reality and what you don't want. Instead allow yourself to focus on thinking about what you do want, such as:

- Feeling happy and fulfilled at the end of the working day.

- Having an excited feeling on a Sunday night when you contemplate the week ahead.

- Waking up happy to go to work.

- Working with people who uplift you and inspire you.

- Making a difference to the lives of others.

You might find it helpful to wear a wristband as a reminder, which you use to 'snap yourself out of it' whenever you catch yourself focusing on what you *don't* want and to trigger you to switch your thoughts towards what you *do* want.

2. Use positive words

Each day become a little more conscious of the words you use as you communicate with others, either written or verbally. For example:

- Use only positive language when you're on social media and avoid sending anything out with a negative vibe.

- Try to avoid getting sucked into conversations with family, friends or colleagues about how bad something is, how wrong someone is, how terrible certain situations are.

- Choose words which put you (and possibly the people you are speaking to) into a higher vibration – words which emit joy, peace or love.

- Start to suspend any judgement about a person or situation by putting a five-second pause in and take a deep breath before responding or reacting.

3. Follow your joy

Whilst this whole book is effectively a journey towards following your joy, there are some ways you can start doing that now. What things light you up? What things enable you to lose yourself in or to feel nurtured or blissful? This doesn't have to be on a large or expensive scale to have an impact. For example:

- Allow yourself some time to be creative – whether that's painting, drawing or crafting.

- Learn to play an instrument you've always wanted to play, or reconnect with one you've already learnt.

- Have a relaxing candlelit bath using some high vibration essential oils.

- Watch your favourite box-set on TV in your pyjamas.

- Spend an evening out having fun with your best friends.

- Get out for a walk and take in your favourite landscape.

Give yourself permission to engage in following your joy, seeing it as part of the broader strategy to discover your purpose.

4. Listen to your favourite tunes

Music is one of the most instant and powerful ways to shift your energy. The sounds we hear from an instrument or a voice are themselves pure vibration and they have the ability to directly impact our own vibration.

There are many studies into the positive impact of music on mood, such as a study in 2015 in *The Lancet*[3], which found that there was a reduction in the anxiety and pain experienced by patients who listened to music before, during and after surgery versus those who did not.

Here are a few suggestions:

- Put on your favourite uplifting song and notice how it feels in your body and if you experience any subtle shifts from the beats, the melody or the voice you are listening to.

- Listen to songs with a higher pitch and a faster beat to help you raise your vibration.

- Create a playlist of 'energy shifters' and keep adding to it as you discover more and more uplifting tunes.

- Have a dance at the same time – let go and shake out any negative or heavy energy.

- You may also consider using tuning forks, singing bowls or a gong for the ultimate sound vibration boost.

5. Use an essential oil

Essentials oils are said to hold the highest frequency of any natural substance – particularly the higher-grade therapeutic oils. An essential oil's higher frequency will raise your own frequency and resolve any energetic imbalances. Each one holds a different frequency with, for example, rose having the highest frequency of 320MHz, frankincense with a frequency of 147MHz and lavender with a frequency of 118MHz. Essential oils in the higher frequency ranges tend to influence the emotions, and the lower frequencies have more effect on physical wellbeing.

You can change your vibrational frequency by using an essential oil in a number of ways:

- **Apply to your skin.** Apply a few drops to the crown of your head, behind your ears, to your neck, to your temples or the soles of the feet.

- **Inhale.** Take three deep sniffs of your oil straight from the bottle or by putting a few drops into the palms of your hands and then inhaling. Cup your hands around your mouth and nose and inhale, breathing deeply for as long as needed.

- **Diffuse.** Place a few drops of your oil into a diffuser to disperse the oil into the air.

6. Have a media detox

Whether it's the TV, the newspapers or social platforms, if you consume a lot of media, chances are you are exposing yourself to a low vibration. Many of the messages we are fed are designed to spread fear, draw us into comparison or elicit a judgemental response. This is a sure-fire way to keep us in a low vibration state. If you have a habit of consuming a lot of media, instead challenge yourself to:

- Set a daily time limit or a window when you give yourself permission to check your social media platforms.

- Give yourself a full break from watching, reading or listening to the news for at least one week.

- Make a note of any shifts, subtle or profound, you might experience as a result of these two actions and begin to extend the challenge out by an extra hour and an extra week.

7. Practice acceptance

Acceptance is cited as one of the higher frequency emotions on the vibrational scale. This doesn't mean that you have to *like* a particular thing, person or situation but it does mean that you are at peace with it – for now. And with that peace comes, as Eckhart Tolle describes in his book *A New Earth*[4], 'a subtle energy vibration which then flows into what you do'.

Within the context of your Career Alignment Journey, you could apply this by:

- Accepting your current situation and any challenges you might be facing.
- Accepting a certain person, such as a difficult colleague or boss.
- Accepting what has happened to you so far within your career or your life.

You can do this as an in-the-moment practice – as and when you are triggered by something which you are resisting. Or as part of your Daily Spiritual Practice by using an affirmation such as "I choose to accept my current job for what it is".

8. Connect with nature

Being in nature is a high vibration experience, especially when you are device-free, and you allow yourself to be fully present. Trees give off a natural, grounding and healing energy which can positively affect your vibration. Here are a few ways to connect with nature and get the full benefit of its wonderful energy:

- **Go forest bathing (known as *shinrin yoku* in Japan).** Get out amongst the trees and take your time to become very mindful of the nature you are surrounded by. Use your senses to fully immerse yourself and spend a few moments breathing deeply.

- **Hug a tree.** I know, this may seem very old-school hippy, but open your mind and just give it a try. It will also increase levels of oxytocin which promote happiness and reduce stress.

- **Stand barefoot on the grass.** Take your shoes and socks off and let the positive energy of the earth beneath you enter through your feet and ground you.

9. Use a high vibration crystal

Crystals hold a powerful and stable energy and can influence the less stable energies around them (in other words us!) Working with a crystal simply by holding it in your hand or putting it in your pocket can help you create a more positive frequency to support you on your journey. You may also choose to use a crystal during meditation or place one on your desk or beside your bed.

Here are a few of the higher vibration crystals which I recommend:

- **Clear quartz.** A great crystal for bringing mental clarity and focus.

- **Rose quartz.** The stone of love and great for promoting self-esteem and harmony.

- **Amethyst.** A must-have stone for helping create calm and relieve anxiety.

- **Citrine.** A stone of abundance which also helps transform negative energy and thought.

- **Selenite.** Good for cleansing the vibration in a particular area or within your body.

10. Give gratitude

It is hard to believe that such a simple practice as giving thanks can have such an impact on your vibration, but it does. Simply focusing your thoughts and emotions on what you already have will instantly elevate your vibration and your mood. Just see what happens when you stop for a minute to give thanks for something simple, such as:

- Your senses.

- Your family and friends.

- The job you may already have (the money you earn, your colleagues).

- The food you eat.

- The water that you have access to.

David's story

When David came to me, he was feeling the after-effects of having just left a successful career in marketing working for a well-known supermarket chain. On the one hand he was ready for the change, embarking on a three-month programme of coaching with me. But his energy told me a different story. He was, understandably, filled with emotion and many of our earlier sessions involved tearful moments. Whilst it was necessary to have the release of energy which comes with a good cry, at the same time it was not the right vibration with which to be beginning his journey towards finding and shifting into a new, more fulfilling career.

We acknowledged that there was an element of grief attached to David leaving behind his old job, his old friends and everything that he had achieved. We also acknowledged that this low vibration was not conducive to him making the change he so desperately craved. We began our sessions with some focus on creating new vibration-raising habits, such as regular walks in nature, deep breathing with an essential oil and giving himself permission to follow his joy with some drawing.

The shift of energy which this created was truly transformative. It then led David into opening up much more fully to the rest of the process and attracting the insight and inspiration he needed to know what direction to head next. Within the three months we worked together, David had already started making plans for opening his own design business, which he duly did 6 months later.

Two final things

Before we move on to the next chapter, there are two things I would like to acknowledge. Firstly, if you have experienced a degree of trauma in the past, there may be some deeper healing work which needs to be done. Whilst I do believe wholeheartedly in this spiritual approach I advocate, having seen the impact on my life and the lives of many of my clients, I do also believe in the importance of working with a mental health professional at certain times in your life. I refer you to your intuition and the part of you which knows how best to handle what you may currently be going through.

Secondly, when you raise your vibration, you also start to see things more clearly and certain people, things and places may no longer be in alignment with you. This is a sign that you are upgrading your energy. It may at times be uncomfortable, but it is a necessary part of your transformation. I encourage you to handle those situations with love and acceptance. This will keep you in the higher vibration state you have created.

CHAPTER HIGHLIGHTS

- Everything in the Universe is made up of energy and there are many things which can impact your energy such as your thoughts and your words.

- It is important to become aware of and manage your energy to enable you to transform your circumstances.

- You are *always* attracting – in a high vibration state you will be attracting what you *do* want and in a low vibration state you will be attracting what you *don't* want.

- If you raise your vibration, your search for purpose will become easier.

Journalling questions

Over the next seven days, keep a diary of what specific things or people impact your energy – both positively and negatively. Are there any themes or patterns that you notice?

When thinking about your career or the change you are looking to make, what is your predominant emotional state and where would it be on the vibrational scale?

What specific thoughts or beliefs might have contributed to that?

What things might you have been attracting with the vibration linked to this emotional state, for example circumstances, people, rewards (or lack of)?

Which of the ten suggested ways to raise your vibration are you most drawn to committing to over the next seven days?

*Nature abhors
a vacuum.*

ARISTOTLE

CHAPTER 3:
Creating Space and Connection

If you want to make a profound change and welcome positive new circumstances into your life, you need to create the space for them to enter into. The clarity you are seeking about what your purpose is or what path to take cannot be found within a cluttered mind or a cluttered space.

If your physical space, your diary space or your head space are filled with what you *don't* want, there will be no space left for the Universe to fill with what you *do* want. All you will get is more overwhelm, more frustration, more stress and more confusion.

Alongside making space, it is also hugely beneficial to your Career Alignment Journey to create a deep connection to the Universe and to your Higher Self. If you are on a spiritual path, you may already have this connection, however, it is a powerful step to formally honour this connection by committing to a Daily Spiritual Practice.

With that connection, you open yourself up to the guidance and support of the Universe which will then enable you to discover a new level of clarity on your journey towards living a life of purpose. And not only that but feeling connected will also bestow a sense of calm, ease and expansion – and who doesn't want more of that!

Let's now look at the different ways you can create space and connection in your life so that you can prepare yourself for aligning with your purpose.

1. Creating physical space

We will first explore a couple of tangible ways you can begin creating space:

Clear out the clutter

"When I put my house in order, I discovered what I really wanted to do" are words which the renowned anti-clutter guru Marie Kondo frequently hears from her clients. In her book *The Life-Changing Magic of Tidying*[5], she also references one client who, after a mass clear out of old books, seminar notes and business cards, had since 'leapt headlong into a new life, quitting her job and finding a publisher for her book'.

Having a good clear out helps you see the wood for the trees. It serves as a reminder of what is truly important versus what you may have tried to convince yourself is important. It forces you to let go of any old, outdated desires so that you can let any current, deeper desires shine through. Even just going through your book collection can give you some valuable pointers as to where you might want to take your career.

I had a client a few years ago who, towards the end of our three months of working together, had the call to become a coach. I recommended a book to help him kick-start his new career. Shortly after, he reported back to me (somewhat sheepishly) that he realised he had already bought this very same book some ten years earlier. The clues were already there lurking on the shelves of his office bookcase!

Everything is energy and everything holds a vibration, as we saw in Chapter 2. When you look at your surroundings (your home, your office or your desk), does it put you into a state of inner ease or a state of inner turmoil? Are you soothed or inspired by some of the objects around you or do they instead trigger you or remind you of something or someone you'd rather forget about? Your vibration and what you sense in your body will always give you the answer.

The 'stuff' around us can unconsciously keep us suspended in a state of attachment. A couple of years ago, around the time when I re-launched my coaching business, I received a strong intuitive nudge to have a mass clear out. I realised that there was a ton of stuff I was holding onto which was no longer serving me, other than to block me from expanding into this new phase of my business which I had so craved.

I took a month off and I went through every single room and every single nook and cranny of my house. There were some shocking discoveries – a full set of impressions of my teeth which I had kept for five years was a particular low point! I quickly recognised how I had been blocking my own flow and transformation through my energetic attachments to a whole range of items.

As spiritual teacher and author Tosha Silver so vividly describes in her brilliant book *It's Not Your Money*[6], there were 'symbolic pockets of pus' which needed to be drained for me to start living in closer alignment with my true purpose. The pus was particularly symbolic in my office, where I unearthed stacks of paperwork from my old days in the corporate world. Why was I hanging onto this? Did I fear that one day I might have to go back there? I think on some level I must have. It was time for it to go.

I duly bought a shredder and spent what felt like an entire week in my garage shredding as though my life depended on it. It was hugely cathartic and represented my letting go of the final throws and outdated identity attachment of my old career. The clarity which emerged off the back of this was quite breathtaking. I stepped forward into my new business identity with such conviction that I hardly recognised myself. My writing started to flow more easily and I began attracting new opportunities and more of my ideal clients who could now see and experience the real me.

When you feel more organised in your physical space, you feel more organised in your mind. Plus, the things which you decide to keep will be things which bring you more joy and more clarity and help to raise your vibration. And we've already seen what that can do for your powers of manifestation.

Here are some suggestions on how to approach clearing out your clutter.

- Remind yourself why you need to do this – what is at stake here? How much do you want to become 'unstuck' and move through your crossroads? How good would it feel to have the clarity to take a leap forward into a more fulfilling career? Keep this in focus.

- Be guided by your inner knowing as to what needs to be thrown away and what needs to be kept and where to start your clear out.

- Try and sense the energy vibration of an object when you look at it or hold it. Ask yourself – does it put me into a high vibration state of feeling joyful, peaceful or loving? Or does it take me to a low vibration state of feeling sad, angry or perhaps guilty?

- Ask yourself how each item is serving you. Does it have a genuine purpose or does it inspire or soothe you in some way? Or are you holding onto it through fear or an unhealthy attachment? Does it trigger you by reminding you of an old association or a time in your life you really need to let go of?

- If something triggers you, I recommend that you allow for the emotional release and show yourself some kindness and compassion.

- Pay attention to any clues or themes which emerge which might highlight a hidden desire, such as those from your book collection.

- Recognise how donating anything which you no longer need could bring joy or help to others. Or how recycling means you will be putting things back into circulation.

Carve out a space to work and practice

If the journey of aligning with your purpose is truly important to you, then it deserves a decent vehicle for you to travel in. By this I mean a physical space where you feel comfortable, focused and inspired to do this work – whether that's reading this book, writing in your journal or doing some online research for your next role. Attempting to work through this process in a place where you are going to be frequently distracted or interrupted or where the energy is not conducive to deep reflective work and thinking is only going to hinder your process.

Hopefully, as a result of clearing out your clutter, it should be an easier task now to create a physical space for yourself (if you don't already have one). Having a dedicated room or office is ideal as it is a contained space where you can close the door and control the energy. This may mean clearing out a spare room you've been meaning to clear out for ages. Or changing the purpose of a room which is not currently getting much use.

Equally, if you don't have the luxury of an entire room, then I recommend simply setting aside a section of a room as your 'career alignment space' (or something similar) and setting a new boundary by letting anyone in your household know what it's for and why it's important to you.

Whatever the size of your space, to make it more sacred and high vibration, you might choose to place some of your favourite crystals, essential oils, quotes or talismans on the desk or table and perhaps a lovely plant which can help support your mood and wellbeing.

For me, this space is my summer house at the bottom of my garden. It's a high vibration place where I feel closer to nature and more connected to the Universe. I also place a couple of crystals around my desk and always have an oil such as black pepper to hand.

Similarly, with your Daily Spiritual Practice, which we will look at shortly, having a designated space or an altar sends out a powerful signal that you are serious about it and serves as a daily reminder of the importance of connection. Altars have traditionally been associated with churches and religion, but they are also now being used more in the home as a place of sanctuary and ritual. I was first introduced to the idea of creating an altar by the wonderful spiritual teacher Rebecca Campbell many years ago and it has been truly transformative for me.

Again, your practice space doesn't need to be an entire room to be effective. I have a little sewing table in the corner of my bedroom which is covered with a white cloth and on it sits a Buddha statue, a meditation candle, an oracle card and my favourite crystal.

Having an altar has created a real focal point for my connection practices which, in turn, have enabled me to live out my purpose more and more each day.

2. Creating diary space

Often, when clients come to me, they are heavily burdened by the busyness of their lives and all their responsibilities. They have been attempting to make changes by stealing half an hour here or ten minutes there to do some serious thinking or job research. If this sounds like you and you're looking to make a profound change, this is simply not going to cut it. (However, I do acknowledge that certain responsibilities might have needed to take priority for you.)

Aligning with your purpose can take time. But I also believe that it is one of the best investments of your time that you can make. Especially if you have been feeling out of kilter, unfulfilled or questioning why you're here. If you don't set proper time aside for this work, other demands will continue to overtake your diary and, before you know it, you will be no further forward.

When I left my last full-time job in the corporate world back in 2010, I took a five-month career break. The breathing space this gave me to explore what my purpose was (alongside the important process of de-institutionalising myself and letting go of my old identity), proved life-changing. I appreciate that not everyone is currently in a position to do this, but with some careful planning and faith in the Universe, it may be a possibility which is at least worth considering.

In the meantime, let's take a look at how you can carve out some time within your current circumstances so that you can:

• Fully engage with this book and the steps and tools

- Start exploring new career ideas.

- Begin pursuing or reconnecting with your passions.

- Feel calmer and less stressed.

Reassess your priorities

Where does your search for purpose currently rank amongst your life's other priorities? Does it get top billing after you've done all the truly necessary things? Or is it something which you try and shoehorn in after everything and everyone else has been taken care of? If you're reading this book, chances are that finding more fulfilment in your life ranks pretty high. But how much is that actually reflected in your list of priorities, in your daily or weekly to do list?

I want you to imagine a jug, which represents a container for your time. There are three things which can go into the jug: some big rocks which represent your life's top priorities, some pebbles which represent some lesser priorities and some sand which represents the minutia of day-to-day life.

What happens if you fill your jug with the sand or the pebbles first? There is no space for the big rocks. But what happens if you put the big rocks into your jug first? The pebbles and the sand can then fill in the gaps around the rocks. When we make space for our main priorities first, we make space for what is truly important and then the rest can slot in around it.

Take a moment now to identify what your big rocks – your priorities – are. What are your pebbles and your sand? To focus on your priorities more (of which your search for purpose is perhaps one of them), it may require you to make a few changes.

Eliminate distractions and time-draining activities

We live in an 'always on' culture – there are so many people and things constantly vying for our attention. There are so many sources of distraction we are exposed to every day – TV, the news, emails, text messages and of course social media (to name but a few). Some of this may be genuinely important to you, but I am guessing that a whole chunk of it is probably not.

Ask yourself what distracts you and how important are these time-zapping activities alongside your big priorities? When I work with clients on time management, one of the first actions they often take away is to cut down their social media scrolling. Even just twenty minutes less each day adds up to over two hours per week. That's two whole hours which can then be spent focused on their future and making their transformation a reality.

I also recommend setting aside times in the day to respond to any messages. As I am writing this book, my phone is on silent and my emails are turned off on my laptop. I give myself a window to check and respond to any messages when I take my coffee, lunch and afternoon walk breaks.

Delegate

If there are certain tasks either within your life or your work (or both) which are too important to eliminate, one way to free up some time is to delegate. This is a word which, when suggested to my clients, is often met with immediate resistance. I appreciate that there are some tasks which simply cannot be delegated, however this resistance can sometimes be masking other issues which might be helpful to be unearthed such as the need for control.

Trying to do everything yourself, especially when there are

options to delegate, is going to harm your ability to make a career change – as well as your own wellbeing. What tasks could you hand over to someone else which would free up some time for you to focus on your priorities? Could you ask a family member to walk your dog or do some housework for instance?

It can help to view delegation as an opportunity for other people to learn new skills, to give back or contribute in a new way and to raise their own vibration in the process.

Say 'no' more often

How many things do you do that take up your time that you don't really want to do? And how many of those things are you doing out of some sort of obligation rather than them being truly necessary? I can't tell you how many times I've had this conversation with clients where they tell me how much they don't want to go to something such as a family meal or a work get-together but they feel obliged and worry about what others would think if they didn't go. If you are desperate for a change in your career and you don't have a lot of spare time, what is it costing you to go along with such things?

Saying no (where appropriate) is one of the most liberating things you can do. It is scary at first, but the more you do it and the more you take the power back into your own hands, the more confident and motivated you will be to keep doing it. What or who do you perhaps need to say no to? And what might that mean to you in terms of space and energy for your true priorities?

Put time in your diary

This sounds obvious, but it is often overlooked as a strategy for carving out time. Just as you would if you had a work meeting or an appointment, put some time in your paper or electronic diary for your career alignment work and, if necessary, let other people know why this is important. Setting aside a block of time, such as a morning, afternoon or even a whole day, is most effective as you are creating a 'container' where you will be able to stay in that expansive energetic space for longer. If that is too much, and it works better for you with your other commitments, then set aside slots of at least one hour.

I also recommend giving this time a name, to signify its importance to you. I've had clients describe their time as their 'personal transformation day' or their 'future me time'. You might also call it something like your 'purpose hour'.

If you aren't currently employed, then I encourage you to see this work as your job now. Commit to it and show up each day as though you were being paid to do it.

3. Creating head space and connection

When you are on the journey towards finding your purpose, your connection to the Universe is invaluable.

This connection means that:

- You don't have to do it all alone.

- You have 24/7 support and guidance.

- Whatever is or isn't happening for you, you have a way to make sense of it.

- You have a safe harbour you can always come back to, however choppy the waters you are trying to navigate.

- You are in touch with the Divine Source of everything.

- You merge more with your Higher Self – your essence, your spirit or your soul.

In order to form or strengthen this connection (and for true clarity to emerge), head space is needed. Head space away from an overactive mind which might be trying to *think* its way through this. And head space away from the current circumstances which might be consuming all your energy.

If you don't already have one, I highly encourage you to begin a Daily Spiritual Practice so that you can create this head space and connection and open up to a whole new level of support, clarity and calm.

Here are three practices I recommend to begin with.

Meditation

The aim of meditation here is to simply let go of thought. This then opens up the space for you to connect with your Higher Self and with the Universal Consciousness which surrounds you. If you are new to meditation, I recommend you start with a short one-minute practice, described below and build it up slowly over time.

- Either keep your eyes open, softly gazing at an object in front of you, such as a candle, or close them so that you can go within, if it feels safe to do so.

- Focus on your breath and follow it in and out, noticing any sensations.

- Scan your body from head to toe and consciously relax every muscle as you do.

- Be fully present by using your senses to become aware of any sounds or smells.

- Try to sense the presence of your inner light, your essence or your spirit.

- If your mind wanders, gently bring it back to your breathing (and celebrate this awareness rather than getting annoyed with yourself for drifting off).

Let go of any expectations or concerns around whether you are doing it right. Just trust in this practice. And remember that it is a practice in *being* rather than *doing* (and that thinking is also a form of doing!)

Prayer

Prayer is a way of communicating with the spirit realm (be that God, the Universe, the Divine or your spirit guides). There is great power in prayer, both to guide you and enable you to create a stronger sense of connection. Prayer can be used to ask for something, to give thanks for something or to acknowledge or release something.

Some of the things you may choose to pray for to help you on your journey include:

- Courage
- Clarity
- Abundance
- Patience

- Peace
- Trust
- Confidence
- Self-worth

Lighting a candle when you pray can help invoke your connection with the spirit realm. After you've prayed for something, listen out for the guidance, the signs or the intuitive nudges which will be given to you. You may choose to say a prayer before or after your meditation practice or whilst you are out walking in nature or relaxing in the bath. Find what works for you.

Breathwork

Breathwork is the practice of breathing more consciously. It is a quick way to connect with your body and disconnect from your mind so that you can feel more equipped to deal with life and bring in a sense of peace and calm.

Here are a few pointers for a breathwork practice:

- Begin with a simple one-minute daily breathing practice where you take long slow deep breaths from your belly.

- Choose certain points during the day or situations where you 'catch' yourself breathing shallowly from your chest and instead consciously take some slower, deeper breaths from your belly.

- Keep an essential oil by your desk or bed to act as a trigger to take three long, slow, deep inhalations from the bottle.

- If you are feeling anxious or overwhelmed, try the four-seven-eight breath: breathe in for four counts, hold for seven counts, breathe out for eight counts (as if you are blowing a balloon), repeating three times.

- Trust in the power of this practice to calm the nervous system and improve your wellbeing.

I recommend that you use one or more of these three practices (or any other practices you feel drawn to) to form your own unique *Daily Spiritual Practice*. And to see that as an important part of your journey towards aligning with your purpose.

CHAPTER HIGHLIGHTS

- Creating physical space, diary space and head space is essential for true clarity about your career path to emerge and to be able to welcome in new circumstances.

- Strengthening your spiritual connection will bring you much-needed guidance, support, and further clarity on your journey towards aligning with purpose.

- Committing to a Daily Spiritual Practice will provide a solid foundation for you to maintain head space and connection.

Journalling questions

Which rooms or spaces in your home or your office might be holding some stuck energy and in need of a clear out?

What old associations or attachments might you be holding onto which are no longer serving you?

What step could you take towards a clutter-free space in this next 24 hours/week/month?

Where in your home could you designate as your special place to do this work? And for your Daily Spiritual Practice?

What priorities represent your big rocks, your pebbles and your sand?

What current distractions could you start to eliminate? What tasks could you start to delegate? What or who could you say 'no' to?

What container of time will you commit to, to do this career alignment work? (How long for, when and what might you call it?)

What do you choose to commit to as a Daily Spiritual Practice?

What you resist persists.

CARL JUNG

CHAPTER 4:
Letting go of Resistance

Even though you may feel highly motivated by the idea of aligning with your purpose or making a career change, underneath the surface there may also be some resistance lurking which has been holding you back or could hold you back in the future. Or perhaps the resistance is much more obvious and palpable for you.

Either way, this resistance cannot be ignored. Your Career Alignment Journey could be a non-starter or will most likely unravel for you at some point if you do not address this resistance. And that starts by simply *acknowledging* the resistance instead of pushing it down.

The task of letting go of resistance can be deeply triggering. It may challenge you. It may shake you at your foundation. It may make you want to run a mile. But please stick with it. In my experience of supporting clients through varying degrees of career changes, it is through this deeper exploration and release that you will arrive at a place where you can create a truly meaningful and lasting career transformation. Plus, the impact is likely to reverberate positively across other areas of your life too.

Fear and self-doubt can have a hugely detrimental effect on reaching your career goals and finding true happiness and fulfilment at work. You could have the most watertight career change plan in place and be totally clear on where you are headed, but if your mindset doesn't fully support that change then you will likely come across some resistance along the way which will stop you in your tracks.

Be gentle with yourself as you work your way through this chapter. If at any point it feels too much then take a breather, get out into nature or meditate. Or if it stirs things up in connection with a past trauma, you may choose to pause this work and seek the support of a therapist or counsellor and then reconvene. I also recommend that you grab your journal to let out any unwanted thoughts and feelings which emerge as we go along. And surround yourself with things which nurture you such as a crystal, a candle or your favourite cosy blanket.

Whilst this chapter forms part of *Preparing The Way*, it may also be something which you choose to come back to as you get further into the book. You may notice that resistance emerges as you work through the other chapters or as you shift into the action phase. Tune into what works best for you and when. As long as you confront the resistance, the timing of it matters less.

What are you resisting?

If you are currently feeling 'stuck' then it is likely that you are resisting something and that your energy is blocked. Some of the most common areas of resistance I witness in my coaching practice in relation to changing career or finding greater purpose are:

- Resistance to change.

- Resistance to taking a risk.

- Resistance to coming out of a comfort zone.

- Resistance to letting go of a current job – the people, the money, the status.

- Resistance to letting go of an outer identity.

- Resistance to success.

Take a moment now to consider what you might be resisting. How does that resistance feel in your body? How might it be holding you back from making the changes you so desperately want to make? I invite you now to make some notes in your journal.

To identify and let go of any resistance, we will now explore two interconnected concepts: recognising the Ego Self and reframing limiting beliefs.

Recognising the Ego Self

The definition of the Ego Self which I use is simply the sense of identity you derive from *outer* things such as:

- Your body and appearance.

- Your job title.

- Your roles (mother, father, carer, organiser).

- Your wealth or status.

- Your people (friends, connections, people you follow).

- Your history (perceived successes or failures).

- Your health (an illness or condition).

- Your thoughts (any fears, judgements, beliefs).

- Your personality or character traits.

The Ego Self is neither bad nor wrong. However, left unchecked, it can have a debilitating impact on your search for happiness at work and on your life generally. I see this all the time in my coaching practice when clients first come to me. Once they open their eyes to the existence of the Ego Self it can often create an immediate shift.

You might experience your Ego Self through an 'inner critic'. The inner critic is that voice inside which tells you that you aren't good enough or haven't done something right. It can show up when you're looking to make a career change by telling you things such as:

- You're not ready yet to take on this new role.

- You don't have what it takes to make this career change.

- You don't deserve to find happiness at work.

Often the Ego Self (and the inner critic) can become even more evident the closer you get to realising your dreams and it can actually be a sign that you are on the right path. The key is to recognise it for what it is (that is, fear) and to accept it as a passenger alongside you on your Career Alignment Journey without letting it get into the driving seat.

Characteristics of the Ego Self

For you to become aware of when the Ego Self has been activated, it is helpful to first identify some of its specific traits. Here is a list of some of the characteristics of the Ego Self. See if any of these resonate with you.

Identifies with
Outer tangible things (job title, appearance, wealth)

How it feels in the body
Heavy, constrictive, tight, closed

Focuses on
Past and future
What others think/expect
Details
Failure

Favourite words and phrases
I/me/mine, I should, what if

Likes
Control, status, being right

Skills
Getting own thoughts across
Judging
Worrying
Overthinking
Grasping
Holding onto things

Beliefs
There isn't enough to go around (scarcity)
Other people's opinions are more important than my own
I am not good enough

Driven by
Competition and comparison

Consequences
Anxiety, depression, stress

Born out of
Fear

At the root of all of these traits is *fear*. One of the quickest ways for you to sense check whether you are thinking or acting from the Ego Self is to ask yourself, "Is this decision or choice coming from a place of fear?" The Ego Self can and will attempt to keep you safe. Safe from criticism, from rejection, from other people being seen in a better light than you. But does it *really* keep you safe? And at what cost? (The Ego Self can be very deceptive). How might the desire for safety actually be keeping you small, right now? How might your Ego Self be creating unhelpful stress and anxiety or making you unhappy in your current situation? How much of your current 'stuckness' is rooted in fear?

How the Ego Self can hold you back in your career

Let us now explore more closely how all of this translates within the context of your career and the journey towards greater alignment to purpose. There is a myriad of different ways the Ego Self can run rampage through your working life and hold you back from making the changes you so desperately want to make.

Here are some of the most common ways:

- Placing too much emphasis on what others might think if you make a career change.

- Not feeling worthy of success or prosperity.

- Playing down your gifts so as not to appear arrogant.

- Trying to control everything and getting lost in all the details.

- Competing with or comparing yourself to others at work.

- Being inauthentic or dimming your light just so you can fit in.

- Not wanting to make a career change unless it is 'perfect'.

- Being attracted to (or staying in) a role because of the status you feel it brings you.

- Fearing that you won't get enough clients or earn enough money if you set up your own business.

- Worrying that your career isn't where it 'should' be at your age.

- Thinking that your job is who you are ("I am a lawyer" or "I am a teacher") and that you will be nobody without that job.

Taking identity from your job

Before I started working for myself and before I became a coach, I will admit that a lot of my identity came from my work. When asked, I liked to tell others what I did. It felt like there was a certain level of kudos attached to me saying "I am a buyer for Sainsbury's." I didn't realise at the time but it was my own Ego Self in action. And in many ways it kept me stuck in that type of role and environment for a lot longer than was good for me. I have since realised that my true identity is nothing at all to do with my work, even now, being fully aligned with my purpose.

Conversely, I often work with clients who have a pull towards a particular job or field which they feel would give them a clearer sense of purpose which they then dismiss as they think it lacks kudos, status or respect and that other people won't therefore view them in a positive light.

The key thing here is that you recognise and then challenge yourself if and when you are being drawn towards or away from a particular career choice by your Ego Self. And to try and get out of your own way so that you can connect with work which will make you truly happy.

Transcending the Ego Self

How much would you love to drop or at least 'soften' your Ego Self? What impact might that have on your search for happiness at work or the journey towards greater alignment? The good news is that there is an alternative to the Ego Self. You don't need to stay stuck. And that alternative is the Higher Self.

In contrast to the Ego Self, the Higher Self is the *inner* essence of who you are. It is the deeper, non-physical identity which lies underneath your outer identity, which you might also describe as your spirit, your soul or your Divine Nature. You might imagine your Higher Self to be like a shiny jewel inside which has been covered over with layers of mud (your Ego Self). However thick the mud is, the jewel is ever-present and changeless.

When you recognise your Ego Self but remember that this is not who you truly are and that you have an alternative, you can open up to a new experience of life. Plus, when you recognise the Ego Self within you it enables you to also recognise it within others. This can lead to greater compassion, empathy and forgiveness and make life more harmonious both in and out of work.

If you already have something of a sense of your Higher Self, you might also be conscious of the conversations which can be held between the Ego Self and the Higher Self (or the head and the heart). I frequently witness this with my clients. They will talk passionately from their heart about the business they want to set up or the new job which lights them up they plan to go for. And then, in the next breath, I can almost see those ideas shift up into their head as the Ego Self-induced fear creeps in and they start to talk themselves out of it. We will explore the Higher Self in greater detail in Chapter 8. In the meantime, I encourage you to just stay aware of the Ego Self if and when it is triggered. And of any conversations which might transpire between your Ego Self and your Higher Self.

Reframing limiting beliefs

The second way to let go of resistance is to unearth and reframe any limiting beliefs you may have. Reframing simply means that you express those beliefs in a new way.

A belief is something which you accept as true or real. The key word here is 'accept', which implies an element of choice on your part. Working on your beliefs and separating out the ones you *know* are true from the ones you are merely *accepting* is powerful stuff. Through shining a light on your beliefs, you can truly start to shift your mindset into a space where lasting transformation can take place.

Empowering versus limiting beliefs

In the context of this book and broadly speaking, beliefs are either *empowering* or *limiting*. Empowering beliefs are those beliefs which will propel you forward and support you on your journey. They are positive and life-affirming beliefs, such as: "I believe that I am capable of creating a happier working life for myself" or "I believe I am worthy of a fulfilling and prosperous career."

Limiting beliefs on the other hand are those beliefs which hold you back. They restrict you and keep you small. They prevent you from moving forward. They feel much heavier in the body.

Limiting beliefs come from the Ego Self which, as we know, is fear-based.

What do you believe is possible for you? Do you believe that you can live a happier and more fulfilling life? Do you believe that you are capable of making a successful career change and deserving of the rewards that come from it? Or is there an underlying belief that it won't happen for you or that it's too difficult? Are your underlying beliefs about your career empowering or limiting or perhaps a mix of both?

Common limiting beliefs

Through my one-to-one client work, I have noticed some recurring themes with the limiting beliefs which are presented to me in relation to finding greater happiness at work. Here are eleven of the most common themes:

*   **Identity.** Beliefs linked to who you think you are such as, "My job is just who I am" or "I am not the sort of person who could ever run my own business."

*   **Worth.** Beliefs linked to what you deserve such as, "I don't deserve to have a fulfilling and well-paid job" or "I am not good enough."

*   **What others think**. Beliefs linked to the opinions of other people such as, "If I don't follow the career path my father followed, I will be disowned" or "I need to prove to my old colleagues that I have progressed."

*   **Scarcity**. Beliefs linked to money or things being in short supply such as, "I need to stay in my job because I won't find another one as well-paid" or "There won't be enough clients for me to make a decent living if I work for myself."

*   **Ability**. Beliefs linked to your skills and comparing yourself to

others such as, "I am not as good at my job as my colleagues and could never be as successful as them" or "If I say I am good at something or appear confident, other people will think I am arrogant."

- **Failure**. Beliefs linked to what might happen if you make a change or take a risk such as, "I have failed at setting up my own business before so I will fail again" or "If I make a change in my career and it doesn't work out, I will be a failure and will have let everyone down."

- **Success**. Beliefs linked to what you fear might happen if you were to succeed such as, "If I become successful, my friends and family may not like me as much" or "If I want to run and maintain a successful business, I need to sacrifice my personal life."

- **Responsibility**. Beliefs linked to what you feel you are responsible for such as, "It is my responsibility to make other people happy" or "I must always put the needs of others ahead of my own."

- **Choice**. Beliefs linked to an 'either/or' mindset such as, "I can either have a career which fulfils me or a career with a good salary but not both" or "I have to stick with the career I originally chose and have trained for" or "If I find true happiness in my career then something bad will happen in another area of my life."

- **Perfectionism**. Beliefs linked to the need for things to be perfect such as, "I need to be 100 percent ready before I embark on a new career path" or "My next career move has to be a perfect fit otherwise I shouldn't make a change at all."

- **Age**. Beliefs linked to your age such as, "I am too old to make a career change now" or "At my age I should be high up the career ladder so I can't start again from the bottom."

How to reframe your limiting beliefs

Here is an exercise to enable you to reframe any limiting beliefs you may have. I recommend you set some quality time aside to work through this.

Step 1. Pinpoint your limiting beliefs

You start by pinpointing any limiting beliefs you may have in relation to what you are looking to achieve or change. Take a moment now to think about leaving your current situation, making a career change and finding the happiness you are looking for. Then consider these questions:

- How possible do you believe that is for you?

- What thoughts, feelings or fears arise?

- What do you believe you deserve?

- What do you believe might happen if you left your current job?

You might find it helpful to take another look through the list of eleven common limiting beliefs and tune into what resonates with you. Write down all your limiting beliefs in your journal. It can be very impactful just to see them in black and white. When writing out your limiting beliefs, begin the sentence with "I believe... " For example, "I believe that I don't have what it takes to make a successful career change."

Step 2. Narrow your focus

To create some focus for the rest of the exercise, I want you to pull out just *one* belief. To choose which one to focus on, look at your list of limiting beliefs and tune into how each one makes you feel and the energy behind it. Then consider these questions:

- Which belief leaps out at you as having the most potential to hold you back from getting to where you want to be?

- Which belief do you sense needs a light shining on it the most?

- Which belief feels the heaviest in your body when you say it out loud?

- Which belief triggers the most intense emotional reaction?

Be guided by your intuition and highlight that one belief. We will now focus on that for the rest of the exercise. (You can repeat this same exercise for the other limiting beliefs over time).

Step 3. Acknowledge the source

Often, the source of a limiting belief can be traced back to other people such as family members, friends, an old boss, a school teacher or even society in general. Or it can stem from a specific past experience (within or outside of work). Either way, when you acknowledge the source of your limiting belief, you are then more able to *disconnect* from it. You start to see it as being separate from you. You realise it was never yours in the first place.

Here are some typical examples of the sources of different limiting beliefs:

- The limiting belief mentioned in step one, "I believe that I don't have what it takes to make a successful career change", could stem from an old boss giving you negative feedback.

- A limiting belief that you should just 'stick at' the career which you originally chose could stem from a parent having always been in the same job their whole life.

- A limiting belief that you will never amount to much could stem from being told that by a teacher way back in your school days.

- A limiting belief that you are too old to make a career change may actually be something you hear your friends say.

Take a moment now to consider what the source of this limiting belief is for you.

Step 4. Declare the benefits

As counter-intuitive as this may sound, it could be that your limiting belief has actually been serving you in some way. Whether consciously or unconsciously, your limiting belief may have been bringing you some benefit. I urge you now to declare that benefit and bring it out into the light. It will be much harder to let go of your limiting belief if you don't honour the way in which it has been serving you.

Here are some of the responses my clients have shared with me when I have questioned them on the benefits of the limiting belief, "I don't have what it takes to make a successful career change":

- It has kept me safe within my comfort zone.

- It has saved me having to make the effort to change.

- It has protected me from judgement and criticism if I had made a change and failed.

- It has protected me from the jealousy of others if I had succeeded.

- I have received attention and sympathy from others about my current situation.

- By delaying and overthinking everything it means I will end up making a better decision.

- It has given me the drive to be better and try harder.

Underlying these (and most other) limiting belief benefits is often a debilitating fear which creates an inertia that keeps you stuck.

Now consider what benefit it would bring if you were to no longer have this limiting belief. What would it feel like to finally let go of this belief? What would it change for you? How might it impact your ability to achieve your goal or make a change?

Here are some of the benefits of letting go of the belief, "I don't have what it takes to make a successful career change", which clients have also shared with me:

- A feeling of freedom to move forward.

- Letting go of the shackles that have been weighing me down.

- Excitement of being able to reach my true potential.

- Finally getting out of a situation which has been affecting me for years.

Step 5. Weigh up the benefits

Now that you have identified the benefits of letting go of and of keeping your limiting belief, you can weigh them up against each other. This enables you to make a fully conscious choice about moving past this resistance and assess your level of motivation.

To weigh up the benefits, I want you to now imagine an old-fashioned weighing scale. Place the benefits of keeping the belief on the left weighing scale pan and the benefits of letting go of the belief on the right pan. Where does the balance of the scale tip towards? Are the benefits of keeping the belief (on the left) heavier than the benefits of letting go of it (on the right)? Or does it tip towards the right side? Or perhaps the scale is evenly balanced?

Only you can decide whether you want to let go of this belief or not and how motivated you are to do so.

Step 6. Disconnect from the source

If you do feel ready to let go of your limiting belief, I invite you now to spend a few moments practising a meditation so that you can begin to disconnect from the source. I recommend you do this in a loving and compassionate way towards any other people involved, to keep your vibration high.

- Close your eyes, if it feels safe to do so.

- Visualise yourself physically handing this limiting belief back to the person (or people) from where it came.

- Tell them that you have no use for it any more.

- Alternatively, you may choose to picture yourself cutting an invisible cord which has been supplying the energy for this limiting belief between you and the person involved.

- If the limiting belief stems from an experience, imagine yourself packing everything about that experience into a box and throwing that box into the bin.

- Make a note of any thoughts, feelings or shifts you experience after this meditation.

Step 7. Create a new empowering belief

The final step is to reframe your initial limiting belief by creating a new empowering belief (or affirmation) to replace it with. Here are some pointers on how to do that:

- Simply turn around your limiting belief into the positive opposite of it. For example, "I am not worthy" becomes "I am worthy."

- Alternatively, just listen out for what emerges from your intuition and your Higher Self.

- Use only positive language referencing what you *do* want as opposed to what you *don't* want.

- Write it in the present tense rather than the future.

- Use language which resonates with you, which *feels* right and is exciting to repeat.

- Consider using empowering words such as 'trust', 'choose', 'accept' or 'allow'.

- See if you can incorporate the benefit of keeping the limiting belief you identified. For example, if safety has been a benefit, your new belief might be "It is safe for me to make a career change."

- Write it in a way that is memorable for you so that you can repeat it more frequently and easily. Try not to make it too wordy.

Using the example of the limiting belief "I don't have what it takes to make a successful career change", this could be reframed as, "I am more than capable of making a successful career change" or "I trust in myself to transform my career situation."

Step 8. Work with your new belief

Once you have created your new empowering belief, it is crucial that you don't just end the process there but instead repeat it on a regular basis. This has both a spiritual and a scientific basis for success. Spiritually, it will connect you to the high vibration which is created from the positive emotion it stirs, helping you attract what you are stating in your belief. Scientifically, the repetition of your new belief taps into something called 'neuroplasticity'. This is the ability of the brain to rewire itself in response to certain stimuli and form new neural circuits.

Here are some tips on how to work with your new belief:

- Write your belief out (put it on a Post-it note next to a mirror or somewhere you will see it each day or create a daily reminder on your phone).

- Repeat your affirmation at least five to ten times daily (you might find it helpful to repeat it as part of your Daily Spiritual Practice).

- Don't just repeat the words, but connect with the feeling and the emotion the belief stirs in you.

- You might find it helpful to record yourself saying the belief out loud and then listening to that back repeatedly.

- Repeat your new belief whenever the old limiting belief gets triggered.

- Become aware of how many times you might still be repeating the old limiting belief and make sure you are saying your new belief more often.

- Check back in on your original limiting belief regularly and see what you notice about your feelings towards it. Does it still hold the same weight and intensity?

I recommend that you work with just one new belief at a time to create proper focus then move onto the next limiting belief on your list and repeat this whole exercise.

Aisha's story

Aisha came to me in search of a fulfilling new path having recently quit her twelve-year career as a biomedical scientist. She had lost the motivation for her work and was noticing a steady deterioration in her mental, physical and spiritual wellbeing.

We explored the possible areas of resistance which were holding her back from moving into a more aligned career path in the area she felt most called to work in (spirituality). In just one session, it quickly became evident what the source of that resistance was. Aisha had subconsciously inherited the belief from her father, "If a job isn't essential it isn't deserving of a high salary." This belief had been serving her by keeping her safe from the potential disapproval of her father.

Once she acknowledged this and realised the benefit of letting go of this limiting belief, Aisha then empowered herself through a new belief, "Abundance is mine and is infinite." She was then able to start making plans towards an exciting new career, initially offering tarot readings.

CHAPTER HIGHLIGHTS

- Your Career Alignment Journey may be a non-starter or unravel further down the line if you don't address any resistance you feel.

- Recognising the Ego Self and reframing your limiting beliefs are two important ways to understand and let go of any resistance.

- The Ego Self can hold you back significantly in your career if it is left unchecked.

- It is possible to reframe your limiting beliefs by acknowledging the source and the benefits and repeating a new empowering belief in its place.

PART 2:
AWAKENING YOUR TRIPLE PURPOSE

Introducing the Triple Purpose

Often when the word 'purpose' comes up in conversation, the default context is around what you do for a living. Whenever I have mentioned to anyone that I'm writing a book about finding your purpose, the responses have been along the lines of "I don't feel fulfilled at all in my job, I could do with reading that when it's finished." There is so much focus and attention in society placed on deriving a sense of purpose from the paid work that we do (and 'doing' in general), that it is easy to overlook any other means of deriving it.

Whilst finding your purpose through your work is hugely important, and central to this book, I believe that a *singular* focus on deriving purpose from your work puts unnecessary and often very unhelpful pressure on you and your job – pressure which can be very counter-productive. Plus, it bypasses the other wonderful sources of purpose which are at your disposal in the here and now and which will provide a more enjoyable and powerful route through to your career-related purpose.

The Triple Purpose comprises of your Higher Purpose, your Life Purpose and your Career Purpose. I use a triangle to symbolise the inter-connectedness of all three. As you will see in the coming chapters, living out your Higher Purpose connects you to your Life Purpose in a deeper, truer way. Which, in turn, enables you to live out your Career Purpose with more confidence and conviction. And so on.

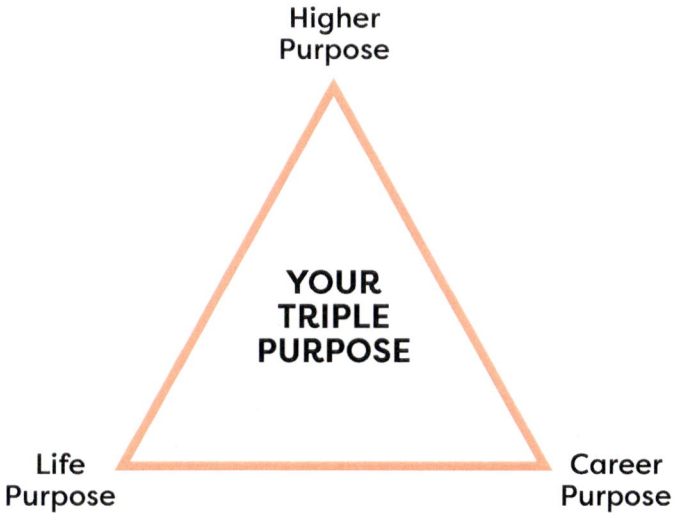

Higher Purpose

YOUR TRIPLE PURPOSE

Life Purpose   **Career Purpose**

It might feel a little unnecessary to work through two other types of purpose before you get to the heart of why you perhaps started reading this book. However, this is not a conventional approach to career coaching, and so I invite you to open your mind and your heart to the journey you are on, knowing that you are right where you need to be.

My own personal experience of focusing on my Higher Purpose and my Life Purpose has led to a greater feeling of balance in my life. It has, in a sense, given me the permission to spend time and energy on things other than work. My life feels more rounded as a result. It has given me a foundation for more connected living and I wish the same for you.

You are here to enable the divine purpose of the Universe to unfold.

That is how important you are!

ECKHART TOLLE

CHAPTER 5:
Your Higher Purpose

Your Higher Purpose is a purpose which I believe we all share, no matter who we are, where we live or what our history or our religious beliefs might be. However, I do also recognise that not everyone may be ready to acknowledge or connect with their Higher Purpose right now. We are all at a different stage in our evolution as a spiritual being in this lifetime.

Your Higher Purpose is to awaken to your true spiritual nature.

Awakening to your true spiritual nature means:

- Looking underneath your outer physical identity and coming to know who you are deep inside at your essence – a Divine Being made of pure light and pure love.

- Seeing yourself as being *part of* the Universe (or God, the Divine, Source, or Consciousness) rather than *separate* from it and acknowledging the oneness of all life forms.

- Sensing the Universal Life Force energy which is both within you and around you at all times.

The word 'awakened' is defined in the Urban Dictionary as 'spiritually aware of the universe and [its] direct metaphysical connection to one's own being and the connection it has to all life forces.'[7]

Whilst there is action implied with the word 'awaken', your Higher Purpose is not so much about 'doing' as it is about 'being'. This can be a challenging concept because, as mentioned previously, we relate so much of our purpose to *doing*.

Being, however, is about moment-to-moment presence and connection. It's about going beyond thought, beyond the mind to a place much deeper within. A place where you will find stillness, inner peace and calm. In many ways, you will know that you are living out your Higher Purpose when you are able to experience this calm, stillness and quietness of the heart. Or when you can look at the sky or a tree or a bird and feel the oneness which connects you.

Why connect with your Higher Purpose first

Whilst you may be eager to find your purpose through your career, I encourage you first and foremost to spend some time focusing on your Higher Purpose. Awakening and recognising yourself as that Divine Being of light, as a part of the Universe, as being connected to all that is, can be truly fulfilling in its own right (that is, without it needing to lead to something else). It is deeply profound and, in many ways, there is nothing higher, nothing greater. It brings with it an innate and unquestionable reason for being.

Here are some other ways in which you can benefit from connecting with your Higher Purpose.

You become a channel for the Universe to work through

Once you have a sense of your connectedness to the Universe, you can then see how it is possible for the Universe to express itself through you. You become a channel or a vessel for that expression. As Eckhart Tolle so beautifully puts it, just imagine the Universe as the sun and that you are a ray of sunshine which emanates from it.

This is hugely significant on your quest for finding more purpose as your work then becomes a vehicle for a deeper mission and thereby more intensely fulfilling. Not only that, but as a channel, the Universe will guide and empower you to carry out the work which it has sent you to do.

We will look at how to act as that channel in the next chapter on Life Purpose, but for now the important point is simply to *recognise* yourself as a channel.

You connect with the Source of everything

When you are connected to the Universe, you are connected to the Source of everything (money, jobs, clients, love, light). This will enable you to live more abundantly, from a place of trust. You will be part of the flow. You will have a place to replenish and fill up your own well.

Again, this is also highly significant as part of your Career Alignment Journey. From that place of connection and fullness, you will have so much more to share with others to enable you to carry out your Life Purpose and your Career Purpose.

Imagine now (or through meditation) that in connecting to

Source, you are effectively plugging yourself in to a virtual power grid. This enables you to turn your own inner light on which will also be seen and felt by everyone around you. Activating your own light first is vital if you want to make an impact in the world and illuminate the way for others through your work.

You connect with a deep sense of self-worth

When I work with clients, the topic of low self-worth often presents itself. And it holds more people back from finding fulfilling work than any other thing.

On a spiritual level, as a Divine Being, you are already worthy, whole and complete. You don't need a job or a relationship or anything in the outer world to justify your existence. You have come into this world for a much deeper reason than to merely perform a role or a function in this world. You are an expression of the Universe and the mere fact that you were born means that you are here for a reason. Your spirit is on a journey and it has taken up residence in your physical form so that it can evolve through your human existence.

From this stable and grounded place anything is possible. You realise that you are worthy of experiencing the joy of a career which truly lights you up. You start to open up to the abundance and prosperity which you previously thought was only available to other people. You stop defining yourself or your chances of success in relation to your personal history, your family or your circumstances.

Other powerful benefits

There are several other powerful benefits in connecting with your Higher Purpose first:

- You let go of grasping for fulfilment and meaning solely from your work.

- You move into a higher frequency state which will help you to attract what you want to you.

- You start to positively impact others just by your presence.

- You will be able to hear your calling (by being tuned in to the Source of the call).

My awakening journey

I first began properly awakening to my own true spiritual nature back in 1998 when I was working in Palm Beach, Florida. Surrounded by an extreme of wealth and materialism, I had an intense inner pull to discover a deeper meaning to life. I began reading the works of Wayne Dyer and books on Buddhist philosophy in an attempt to figure things out. The pull was too loud to ignore, even though I felt very alone out there in my desire to explore my true identity.

And then again in 2010 when I followed my instincts to take a career break in Australia, I awakened further. Having left the confines of my corporate career once and for all and also having carved out the necessary time and head space, I accelerated the process of understanding who I was beyond my job title and my CV.

It wasn't an easy process at first. In fact, I spent the first two weeks of my career break wondering around the shopping malls and the beaches of Sydney's eastern suburbs wondering what on earth I had done. I was in, what William Bridges in the book *Transitions*[8] called a 'neutral zone'. A sort of no man's land in between my old outer identity and my emerging, true spiritual identity. I had to get back to basics and to strip back all the outer trappings which had been masking over my Divine Nature. This eventually led me to where I am today – doing work in total alignment with my being and a deep sense of purpose.

For the two years preceding me writing this book, I have been largely focused on my Higher Purpose. It wasn't something I had planned as such, but rather something I was called to do by my Higher Self. In the Autumn of 2020, I had just created my first online coaching course and was eager to get it out into the world. I invested in a business coach to help me put some sales and marketing strategies in place and launch my course into the marketplace. I joined the local Chamber of Commerce to start forging links with businesses I could sell my course to. And I began developing some online group coaching workshops.

This was supposed to be me taking my business to the next level. But something inside didn't feel right. I questioned whether this was just resistance to coming out of my comfort zone and just my Ego Self trying to keep me safe. However, it felt like something deeper was going on.

Alongside the traditional business growth strategies, I had also been hugely drawn to gaining a deeper understanding of the work of Eckhart Tolle and so I enrolled on his course, *Conscious Manifestation*. The main message being that we must connect with our being and our inner purpose first, to manifest from a place of true power. I was deeply fascinated by this approach, even though it was so contrary to the conventional methods of growing a business.

Around the same time, I had another piece of guidance sent to me from the Universe which hit me square between the eyes. As a member of spiritual teacher Rebecca Campbell's *Rise Sister Rise Sisterhood*, I was sent an oracle card which she had pulled personally for me, totally out of the blue. The card was called '*Double Mission*' and its meaning was around how my mission is firstly to raise my own consciousness so that I can then enable other people to raise theirs. I couldn't ignore this. And so, at that point, I recognised that the work to do was on my own inner self (my Higher Purpose) rather than any outer work. Growing my business had to begin deep within me.

Following this intuitive guidance, I had a strong urge to 'pull back' from the outer world and stop doing things I thought I 'should' do. I let go of all my plans and goals for my online course. I cancelled my membership with the Chamber. I stopped pushing myself to create group coaching programmes. I simplified my business to focus on what brought me the most joy (my one-to-one client work) and create the space to truly embrace my Higher Purpose.

As part of my focus on my Higher Purpose, my Daily Spiritual Practice became non-negotiable. I started going out for more mindful nature walks. I started to understand the true meaning of meditation. I started being led by peace instead of the desire for more. I started recognising the abundance I was already living in. I started becoming truly conscious – of my thoughts, my energy, my ability to be present. I started to exchange control for trust. I started to feel myself as part of the Universe itself. And I started to feel the connection to something bigger which I longed to serve.

As a result of all of this I began to experience a new level of inner peace and calm. Many previous experiences of anxiety and panic all but disappeared. I reconnected to my work in a way which I didn't even know was possible, re-launching as a spiritual career coach and finally working with clients who I truly resonate with. My writing started to flow more, as if a tap had been turned on. I began to understand how I could serve others by being a *channel* for the Universe to work through. I recognised my Ego Self at work more and, instead of being led by it and thinking I was the one having to do it all alone, I started to let go and trust.

The impact of my work and the results clients achieved seemed to improve measurably. I started receiving and tuning into intuitive messages and guidance much more easily. My vibration was noticeably higher and I began to have a far greater sense of what and who was in alignment with me. To sum it up, it has been truly life-changing to focus on my Higher Purpose!

And so, I wholeheartedly encourage you to do the same by staying open to your own inner whispers, nudges or when things don't feel quite right. By making the time and space to focus on your Higher Purpose. And by daring to open yourself up to becoming a channel for the Universe to work through. I promise you it will be worth it.

Awakening through life's challenges

It is possible that you may discover your Higher Purpose and awaken through an act of grace. This is when the Universe spontaneously and unexpectedly presents you with the opportunity to awaken through a change of circumstances. Things are taken out of your hands. This change is often accompanied by a level of discomfort, struggle or some sort of crisis.

A classic example of this in a career context is redundancy. Sometimes, clients approach me either immediately before or after being made redundant. Once the initial shock, rage or panic has worn off, the potential of their job loss as an *opportunity* suddenly dawns on them. Conversations turn from, "How could they do this to me and what am I going to do now?" into "I would never have had the guts to do this myself", and "It's the best thing that could have happened to me." Suddenly, they are *forced* to re-evaluate their life, to remember that their job is not who they truly are and to go within. There is an opening.

If you are currently going through a redundancy, I wholeheartedly encourage you to see the opportunity which could lie underneath this challenge. Rather than going headlong into a fresh job search, if you can, try and allow yourself to be awakened and connect with your Higher Purpose. Trusting Divine Timing can be hugely helpful in regaining perspective here too.

Another way in which your Higher Purpose can emerge by an act of grace is through illness. I had a client come to me a few years ago as she was feeling very unfulfilled in her career and was longing to quit her corporate job and work for herself doing something she truly loved. She was holding herself back from making the career change she knew she needed through fear of judgement and letting go of her steady income. Then, halfway through our coaching programme, she developed breast cancer. Needing to refocus her time and energy on her health and recovery, we took a break from our sessions.

When we reconvened and she updated me on her life and how she was feeling, I sensed that on some level she had awakened. Her Higher Self was shining through in a new and more obvious way than before. Her illness had forced her to reassess her entire life and there was much greater clarity both on the path ahead and on what was no longer serving her. She finally started recognising her own wellbeing needs and finally felt empowered to quit her job of fifteen years, which was hugely liberating for her. This awakened state brought her a new sense of purpose and connection and paved the way for the next step on her career path.

My biggest awakening happened following the very sudden death of my dear Mum. This was an act of grace like no other. The death of a loved one truly shakes your foundations and makes you look at life from a new angle. It helped me witness close up that whilst our physical form or outer self is temporary, our spirit is eternal. I feel her light, her love and her spirit with me at all times, especially as I write this book. It has proved to me beyond doubt that we never truly cease to exist. We just change form.

My Mum's passing has forced me out of an attachment to who I *thought* I was (my body, my work, my name, my history) into a full recognition of myself as an eternal spirit residing in a human form. My Higher Purpose (along with my Life Purpose and Career Purpose) has been made clear to me as a result of this most difficult of life events and for that I am truly grateful.

Had I not already experienced an awakening myself, I am pretty sure I would not have written this book. I now recognise my true spiritual nature and feel the connection to my Higher Purpose each and every day. And the fulfilment, the contentment and the inner peace which I now have access to as a result s exactly why I wanted to share this with you. Because at the heart of most people's search for purpose is a desire for greater fulfilment, contentment and inner peace. And you can start accessing that now.

Of course, this is not to suggest that you need a redundancy, an illness or the death of a loved one in order to awaken. It is more about recognising the gift and the opportunity which lies within life's challenging circumstances and seeing them as a part of your journey towards greater purpose and fulfilment.

Tools to enable an awakening

You may be reading this book having already awakened to some degree and you may already be experiencing this connection to Higher Purpose on a regular basis. If you haven't yet awakened, I encourage you to just be open to exploring your inner being, to give it time and head space and to create the right conditions for an awakening to occur. We will now look at some ways in which you might do just that.

1. Nature

I believe that nature provides us with the most beautiful and powerful means to connect with our own essence and the oneness of the Universe. The existence of nature is proof of the existence of the Universe (whether through a bird, a tree or the sky). Take a walk out into nature and see if you can sense the omnipresent Universal Life Force which resides within everything you see. Recognise that the same Universal Life Force which enables the seasons to change and the flowers to bloom also resides within you. Even if you can't get outside, take a look out the window at the sky and see if you can connect that way.

2. Meditation

The essence of meditation is about going beyond thought and connecting within. It is such an important core practice. What meditation allows you to do is experience the gap between thoughts where there is total stillness and space. And in that stillness and that space is where you can tune into your true spiritual nature and connect with the Universal Life Force which surrounds you.

This space also provides the opportunity to take a step back from your thoughts and, rather than getting caught up in them or taking your identity from them, to recognise yourself as the *observer* of those thoughts.

Next time you meditate, see if you can sense the stillness and the presence which is within you and around you, even if just for a few moments.

3. Candlelight

For me, there is nothing quite like the light of a candle to remind me of my own essence and the consciousness which surrounds me. There is something otherworldly and hypnotic about a flame which transports me to that deeper place within. There is also a secondary element to the candle symbol which is seeing your role as a bringer of light to others (something we will explore in Chapter 6).

Have a go and see if you can connect too:

- Light a candle and sit with it in a quiet space.

- Look directly at the flame and, as you do, let go of any thoughts.

- Let it reflect back to you your own inner light (your essence) which is burning bright.

- Repeat a mantra, such as "I am the light."

- Recall this experience throughout the day to remind you of your essence.

4. Prayer

Here is a suggested prayer for you to use to help you connect more directly with your Higher Purpose:

Dear Universe,

I wish to connect with my Higher Purpose and to deeply understand my true spiritual nature.

Help me to peel back the layers of who I think I am, so that your light can shine through.

Help me to know myself as a Divine Being who is already worthy, whole and complete.

I ask for your guidance to be seen and felt, so that I may make more aligned choices.

I ask to feel your presence around me and within me.

I am open to becoming a vessel for your love and your light.

I am ready.

5. Affirmation

You could also work with an affirmation to help you connect to your Higher Purpose, such as:

- I am light and I am love.

- I am already worthy, whole and complete.

- I open up to becoming a channel for the Universe to work through me.

Repeat one of these several times a day until you feel it has fully integrated. You might choose to include it as part of your Daily Spiritual Practice.

6. Presence

Whenever you are truly present in the moment, you are able to access and experience your true spiritual nature and become aware of the presence of the Universe. You can do this throughout the day, at any time. Allow yourself to have moments where you are fully present so that you can let this Universal Life Force come through you and connect you with your inner being.

You can incorporate the practice of presence wherever you are:

- At your desk

- In the supermarket queue

- On a plane or in a car

- In bed

- In the garden

- Out for a walk

See if you can connect with that presence in a whole range of situations. This truly is a transformative practice which will also enable you to feel calmer and more peaceful.

CHAPTER HIGHLIGHTS

- In addition to your work-related purpose (your Career Purpose) there are also two other sources of purpose which you can access now: Your Higher Purpose and your Life Purpose.

- Your Higher Purpose is to awaken to your true spiritual nature and is less about doing and more about being.

- Your Higher Purpose can be a source of fulfilment in and of itself.

- Focusing on your Higher Purpose first will empower both your Life Purpose and your Career Purpose.

- By seeing yourself as part of the Universe and connecting with the Source of everything, you can become a channel for love and light.

Journalling questions

To what degree do you currently recognise your true spiritual nature?

What would change for you if you were to have a stronger foundation of self-worth?

What would change for you if you were to see yourself as a channel for the Universe to work through?

What challenges are you experiencing which might be an opportunity for you to awaken more to your true spiritual nature?

Which tool do you choose to try over the next seven days to help you to connect with your Higher Purpose?

Make me a channel of your peace.

Where there is despair in life let me bring hope.

Where there is darkness, only light.

And where there is sadness, ever joy.

PRAYER OF SAINT FRANCIS OF ASSISI

CHAPTER 6:
Your Life Purpose

Discovering your purpose is not just about waiting until you have made a big life or career change. It's also about looking for ways to bring more meaning into your life within the here and now. It's about drawing on the connection to your Higher Purpose and seizing the daily opportunities to bring that connection to life in the outer world in a tangible way. If Higher Purpose is all about 'being' then Life Purpose (and Career Purpose) is all about 'doing'.

Your Life Purpose is to be a channel for the love and light of the Universe.

Being a channel means allowing the Universe to work *through* you to bring more love and light into the world. This means channelling the gifts of kindness, forgiveness, truth, peace, compassion, connection, gratitude, understanding, joy, hope and consciousness.

As with Higher Purpose, I believe this definition of Life Purpose is also something which we collectively share. It is your choice as to whether you show up to that purpose. Your current life or career circumstances don't really have a bearing as this purpose can still be lived out even on the smallest of scales and in the most limited of situations. Through simply projecting a high vibration or through the practice of prayer, you can become a channel for love and light without even coming into contact with anyone.

The essence of your Life Purpose is that you are guided by love and by your Higher Self in your actions and by living in a higher vibration state. That is not to say that you need to try and act like a saint in order to fulfil your Life Purpose! You are an evolving spiritual being having a human experience. And the human experience is challenging. But, through your Life Purpose, it is possible to connect the two worlds (the spiritual and the human). You acknowledge your Divine Nature and you carry out the work which the Universe needs you to do in human form.

As I was writing this chapter, something serendipitously dropped into my mailbox from the Susan Jeffers Organization, the author of the self-help classic, *Feel The Fear And Do It Anyway*. It was a monthly newsletter with excerpts from her work and one passage leapt out at me. She wrote 'Within every one of us lives a place of light and love that I call the Higher Self. Perhaps hurtful life experiences have built walls making it invisible. Nevertheless, the place of light and love is always there!'⁹

Why connect with your Life Purpose

There are several reasons why this way of viewing your Life Purpose is significant both within your life generally and also in the context of aligning with more purposeful work.

What you give to others you also give to yourself

As with your Higher Purpose, living out your Life Purpose can bring fulfilment in and of itself. For example, seeing the difference you can make to someone's life just through offering a smile or an understanding ear. In giving to others, you too can receive. And ultimately, if it is fulfilment which you are searching for through your work, why not access it outside of work too?

Connecting with your Life Purpose in this way can have a powerful effect both on your own day-to-day happiness and on your ability to attract the right circumstances to enable you to align with your Career Purpose. When you act from a place of love, you raise your own vibration. And from that higher vibration state, you can then line up with the vibration of what you want so that it then comes into your experience.

Conversely, when you hang on to resentments or continually judge others, you keep your vibration very low. And this is going to stop you from lining yourself up energetically with what you want to attract.

Acting as a vessel for love and light not only serves the other person but it also serves you. But you must come from a place of fullness to be able to have something to offer, which is why your Higher Purpose is so important to connect with first – so that you can plug into the ultimate Source of that love and that light.

You tap into a powerful energy stream

When you carry out your Life Purpose and you offer something to the world purely for the joy of it, you connect with a powerful energy stream. This energy stream runs through both your Life Purpose and your Career Purpose. Tapping into it now through your Life Purpose will signal to the Universe that you are open and ready for more, through the work that you do. The Universe will then find more opportunities for you to connect to that energy stream, particularly if you listen to your intuition for the messages and the nudges.

You can test the waters for your Career Purpose

Through your Life Purpose you open your mind and your heart to something which could eventually become your Career Purpose. In a sense, you get to 'test the waters' to see if this resonates with you and provides you with the fulfilment you are looking for. Connecting to your Life Purpose through, for example, volunteering to support the homeless or letting your creativity shine by attending an art class, can act as a stepping stone towards an even greater expression of your purpose.

The world needs you!

Even as someone who doesn't watch or read the news, it is glaringly obvious to me how desperately the world needs more love and more light. On top of the global phenomenon of war, racism and a recent pandemic, as humans we have also become obsessed with our outer identity and the need to compare and compete. We have become driven by the constant desire for more. We have a dizzying array of responsibilities to juggle. In short, life for many has become more complicated, more overwhelming and more disconnected from true meaning than ever before.

And the only way we are going to turn this ship around is if we all see it as our own personal responsibility to contribute towards a more awakened and enlightened planet. To bring more consciousness into the world and become a beacon of light to enable others to do the same. In doing so, we will create a powerful ripple effect which extends across our homes, our cities and our world.

Five steps to activate your Life Purpose

Here are some suggested steps to take to activate your Life Purpose.

Step 1. Connect to the Source of love and light

The first step in living out your Life Purpose involves connecting yourself to the Source of that love and light (the Universe). You can connect to the Source through the practices I shared with you in Chapter 5. For example, a simple morning meditation practice of even just five minutes where you imagine 'plugging in' to the Universe and to the stream of love and light coming in through your crown chakra. At the end of your meditation, you can also set an intention for the day such as "Today, I intend to be a channel of love and light for all whom I come into contact with."

Step 2. Think consciously

Everything begins with a thought – every word you speak, every choice you make, every emotion you feel and every action you take. Carrying out your Life Purpose involves becoming *acutely aware* of the thoughts that you think. And then, from this place of awareness, you can make a choice to act as that channel of love and light by consciously changing your thoughts (where necessary) to ones which foster more kindness, more forgiveness, more truth, more peace, more compassion, more connection, more gratitude, more understanding, more joy, more hope and more consciousness.

Remember too that your thoughts hold a frequency and that others will be able to pick up on that frequency without you even saying a word. What frequency do you want to be emitting? In order to think more consciously, it may also be helpful to connect with your Higher Self as your Higher Self is the part of you which is naturally guided by love.

Step 3. Communicate consciously

Listening

Conscious communication begins with listening, deeply. It involves holding the space for the other person to express themselves without interjecting or immediately sharing your own version of events. It involves allowing the other person to feel properly heard. And it is one of the greatest gifts you can give to another person, even without you giving a response. Although often, from this place of deep listening, you may find that you actually have *more* to offer if you do give a response, as more insights and intuitive thoughts will have had the space to come through.

Speaking and writing

Conscious communication is also about speaking and writing from a place of love instead of from a place of fear. It means pausing before you respond and speaking words which promote more truth, kindness, compassion and acceptance instead of judgement and hatred.

It doesn't mean that you have to agree with someone's point of view or condone negative behaviour. Speaking or writing consciously also means voicing the truth. Even if you are having to communicate something difficult or say no to someone, you can set an intention to do so with love and in alignment with

Source. The words you speak and write hold a vibration. When you communicate with a positive intention, it will be received accordingly by the other person.

Next time you are communicating with someone, check in on the energy behind the words you are writing or speaking and ask yourself whether they are charged with anger, envy, fear or judgement. See how you might be able to communicate the same message with a lighter energy.

Step 4. Act consciously

There are many ways within day-to-day life in which you can spread love and light through your actions. You can spread love and light to friends, family, strangers, people in need, those who serve you, your community, animals, Mother Nature or even to all living beings on the planet.

These are some of the many ways you can act consciously and share your Life Purpose:

- Offering support or comfort to someone in need

- Practicing acceptance towards someone who you find challenging

- Offering a simple gesture of kindness

- Giving someone your time

- Practicing forgiveness and showing understanding

- Creating connections with others

- Protecting nature

- Managing your consumption

- Showing gratitude

- Encouraging or inspiring others

- Sharing beauty, joy and laughter

Step 5. Become truly present

I want to give a special mention to being present as it holds great power to transform your life. Being truly present is not about thinking, communicating or acting (although it can be brought into all three). It's about suspending thought, speech and action and accepting the moment just as it is. In doing so, you have a clearer connection to Source so that the love and light can be accessed and felt. There is less outer 'noise' and clutter which enables you to hear the messages the Universe wants to communicate through you.

In a state of true presence, you are able to raise your frequency and have something positive to offer other people (and the planet at large) through the energy which you emanate. Even people who have decided to pull back from the outer world and live in isolation can have an impact on the world purely through their energy.

Ten ways to live out your Life Purpose

I'd love to share with you some specific and very accessible ways in which you can live out your Life Purpose. See which one(s) resonate with you and give them a go.

1. Nurture the wildlife in your garden

A couple of months ago, I noticed a queen bee struggling to move in my garden. I grabbed a saucer and made a little sugary solution for her and put it on the garden next to her and left her to it. When I returned an hour or so later, she had replenished her depleted energy levels and flown off. I can't tell you the amount of joy this brought me.

There are countless ways we can spread more love and light by nurturing the nature which surrounds us. The simple act of feeding the birds or making sure they have some fresh water to drink can connect you to your Life Purpose in an instant.

2. Volunteer

Sharing some of your time to support a charity or a cause is a very life-affirming thing to do. Especially when it directly provides you with an opportunity to spread more love and light to another living being – whether that's a child, a homeless person, a woman in a domestic abuse situation, an animal or even Mother Earth.

I recently began volunteering for a charity which aims to stem the experience of loneliness in the elderly. I pay a weekly visit to a wonderful lady in her late eighties called Jean. This was in direct response to me wanting to live out more of my Life Purpose in a way which was entirely separate from the work that I do. As well as being deeply fulfilling, I also feel this has opened me up on a new level to the Universal flow of love and light which can also now be felt more within my work.

3. Practice acceptance towards someone who triggers you

Often in life there is someone who pushes your buttons and triggers a negative response, be that a thought, a conversation or an action. Whilst it may feel like a big stretch to want to spend a lot of time with this person or start loving them unconditionally, the practice of acceptance could offer you a baby step and another opportunity to bring more love and light into the world. I believe that challenging people and situations are presented to us as an opportunity for us to grow and evolve.

Acceptance, as well as being one of the higher vibration states on the frequency scale, is a practice which can bring you greater inner peace too. Next time you get triggered, instead of your normal response, take a breath, pause and connect with the energy of acceptance and see what changes for you.

4. Create more connection amongst your friends

Being forced to disconnect from family, friends and colleagues during the pandemic left many people feeling bereft and depressed. The remembrance that, as human beings, we have an innate need to connect with others hit many of us square between the eyes.

Instead of waiting for others to get in touch to arrange a coffee or to host the next get together, why not take on that role yourself and see it as part of your Life Purpose? As another opportunity to spread the love and the light.

I had a client who clearly played this role within their family. Every now and then, she used to resist it and feel deeply triggered, wondering why no-one else was seeing it as so important to get people together. Once she fully accepted this as part of her purpose, she was able to embrace the role and enjoy each occasion even more.

5. Offer a smile to a stranger

Back in the mid 2000s when I worked for Sainsbury's, I had a daily commute into London on the Tube. Every day I would get onto the same carriage at the same time, surrounded by the same fellow commuters. And nobody would speak. This blows my mind when I look back now. I often wonder what would have happened if I had offered a 'hello' or a little knowing smile – even if just to acknowledge the other person's existence and that we are all in it together.

Often, as was my case above, we can wait for the other person to smile or say hello first, for fear of it not being reciprocated or of us appearing somewhat strange. There is no telling what the ripple effect could be of you sharing such a simple exchange. A smile is an easy way of sharing a little of the Universe's light and it costs nothing. It could be just what the other person needs.

6. Use social media for conscious communication

Social media has great power to divide and separate and to promote hatred amongst the collective. It also has great power to connect and to promote love. Through conscious communication, we can all play our part in making social media a vehicle for greater love and light and to stem the flow of negativity.

It might be just one post which you put out which shows someone support or encouragement or shares a message which is rooted in love. It might also be about the message you choose *not* to send which may have been born out of fear or judgement. Next time you are on social media, take a moment to reflect on how you can communicate more consciously and how that might impact others and the world around you.

7. Say a prayer for someone in need

Sometimes we may be unable to do very much on a practical level to help another person in need, for example if they are sick or in a challenging situation. But we can ask for the assistance of the Universe for them. Through prayer, we imagine the best outcome for another person. We offer a high vibration and the possibility of healing and change. This is powerful stuff and another way in which we can act as a vessel for the Universe.

My Mum was well-known for her nightly prayer list which always had at least 25 people on it. She always believed in the power of prayer and in the possibility of a miracle. This is another great gift that we can give to others as part of our Life Purpose.

Here is an offering of a prayer to get started.

Dear Universe

I ask for your support for...

May you guide and support them through this challenging time.

And bestow your love and light onto them so that they may heal.

And move forward positively on their human journey.

I offer this up, knowing that with you all things are possible.

8. Show gratitude to those who serve you

If there was one wonderful thing which arose from the pandemic, at least here in the UK, it was the outward expression of thanks for those who serve us. For several weeks, many of us dutifully came out of our houses at 8pm on a Thursday evening to clap for the 'key workers' who kept our country running and looked after the sick. It was the most moving experience of collective gratitude many of us have ever witnessed.

There are opportunities every single time we interact with someone who is serving us in some way to continue to show gratitude. For some people, it might be the only thanks or praise they ever receive. A simple 'thank you' goes a long way. Whether that's the person on the checkout in the supermarket, the barista who prepares your coffee or the receptionist who books your appointment with the doctor. Or you may choose to go the extra mile and write a letter or email to a person's manager. This was something else my Mum used to do and she was always amazed by how little people received such messages and what a difference it made to that person's life.

9. Be kind and patient to your fellow drivers

There is something about being behind the wheel of a car which can make me feel defensive and self-righteous. I can often sense the tension, urgency and even aggression of other drivers too. So much so, it can be hugely challenging to maintain my own sense of calm and inner peace as I go about my journey. People not indicating, going through a red light or cutting me up can often elicit a very low vibration response.

If you can relate to any of this, here's another opportunity to carry out your Life Purpose. What the other road users perhaps need more than anything is something which counterbalances their impatience or rage rather than a response which only serves to exacerbate it.

Simply giving way to other road users, showing them some understanding when they appear to be in a massive hurry or are acting out of their fear-based ego by shouting or cursing is just another way you can bring more love and light into this world.

I recently made a promise to myself that I would choose peace instead of impatience whenever I'm driving. Peace, after all, is one of my top values, so why wouldn't I choose a more peaceful thought whenever I'm in a situation where I feel I need it most? (It's a work in progress!)

10. Pick up the litter

Most mornings before I start my working day, I go for a walk around a beautiful fishing lake near to my house. I feel so fully immersed in nature there and it leaves me with such a warm glow. Whenever I see litter strewn on the banks of the stream and in the bushes, I feel almost personally offended on behalf of Mother Nature. It's easy to take the view that 'it's not my problem' or 'someone else will come and pick it up' as I often do.

As my love of nature has intensified, I have started to see the opportunity for me to take a more active part in protecting and caring for it. And so, I have occasionally begun picking up the litter. I try not to feel angry towards the person who dropped it (also a work in progress) and instead acknowledge the collective responsibility we all have to show love towards this beautiful planet which nourishes us and sustains us.

CHAPTER HIGHLIGHTS

- Through your Life Purpose, there are many ways you can bring more meaning to your life right now.

- Your Life Purpose is to be a channel for the love and light of the Universe.

- The essence of your Life Purpose is being guided by love and by your Higher Self.

- Connecting with your Life Purpose can also open you up to aligning with more purpose within your career.

Journalling questions

In what ways might you currently be living out your Life Purpose?

What benefits might it bring to your life if you were to connect more with your Life Purpose? For example fulfilment, the ability to test the waters ahead of a career change, a sense of calm.

What benefits might it bring to your career if you were to connect more with your Life Purpose? For example, taking the pressure off your new job search, creating a positive energy.

Who do you know who embodies this Life Purpose and inspires you in some way?

Which of the daily opportunities to connect with your Life Purpose appeal the most to you? (Feel free to create a list of your own).

We can change the world and make it a better place. It is in your hands to make a difference.

NELSON MANDELA

CHAPTER 7:
Your Career Purpose

Let's now head into the heart of the book – finding more purpose and meaning through the work which you do – by starting to explore what your Career Purpose is about and the benefits that aligning with it can bring into your life.

Your Career Purpose is
to make a difference in the world
by doing the work you are called to do,
using the gifts you have been given.

On a soul level and on an energetic level, your specific Career Purpose already exists. It is already written. And so, in a sense, this is less about 'finding' your purpose and more about 'aligning' with it. It is less of an external thing you need to search for or try to come up with on your own and more of an internal job of re-connecting with your True Self, listening to your inner voice and releasing any resistance so that you come into resonance with your Career Purpose.

How aligning with your Career Purpose transforms your life

It might be fair to assume that if you are reading this book, you are already somewhat motivated to do the work which will connect you with your Career Purpose. However, as motivation is a key ingredient in taking the necessary action to move you forward, I think it might be worth sharing some of the transformative benefits anyway.

1. Deep fulfilment and aliveness

In my coaching practice, I have witnessed a lack of fulfilment as one of the main causes of unhappiness for people at work. Conversely, when people do the work which is in alignment with who they truly are and they are making the impact in the world which they know they were born for, a whole world of joy and happiness is unlocked. When you are doing the work which you are meant to be doing and you feel it on a cellular level, it comes with a sense of deep fulfilment and aliveness. There is a sort of 'clicking into place' and things just seem to make sense.

2. Inner confidence

It can take great courage to make a career change, especially if it means entering a new sector or working for yourself and putting yourself out there for the first time to attract clients. When you come to understand your work as a mission you have been sent to accomplish, and that you were born to make an impact in the world, you tap into a deep source of courage and conviction. You recognise that it's not about you. It's about the people, the animals, the planet or whatever you end up choosing to serve. You get over yourself and you show up.

3. Enhanced relationships

I don't know one client for whom aligning with their Career Purpose hasn't had a positive ripple effect on their close relationships. It can be challenging for partners, parents, children, close friends and colleagues to constantly hear the moans and groans stemming from an unhappy and unfulfilling career situation. But when you are doing the work you're here to do and living from a higher vibration, others will feel it too and your relationships can't help but benefit.

4. Expansion

When I work with career change clients on identifying their values, 'making an impact' often emerges as being deeply important to them. When you recognise and show up to your Career Purpose, you enable yourself to make a bigger impact and you stop playing small. You stop holding yourself back. You realise you are here for bigger things than perhaps your current situation allows. Your scope of vision expands. You start playing big. And the world needs more people who are doing just that.

5. Improved wellbeing

When you are in alignment with your Career Purpose, fully showing up in the world and feeling more confident, there is a sense of inner ease which accompanies it which can positively impact your wellbeing. Stress levels in people who are doing the work they are meant to be doing are often lower and the higher vibration from feelings of joy and happiness can also keep away many ailments. That's not to say that you can't still overwork when you are fulfilling your Career Purpose (as I know only too well!) I do still recommend boundaries and practices to maintain balance, but there is a different energy behind it. You are working because you want to and because you love it. It comes from a different place.

6. Overcoming challenges

Similarly, when you are living out your Career Purpose, you may still face some challenges. Whether that's sourcing new clients, trying to juggle your work and home life or finding people who buy into your idea for change. But when you are clear on your Career Purpose and you feel it in your bones that this is why you are here, it gives you the determination and the resilience to keep going. Also, if you connect with your Higher Self, you may choose to view the challenges as an opportunity for growth, for you to trust in the Universe even more deeply and to connect with your spiritual practices with even more intent.

Connecting your Career Purpose with your Higher Purpose

When you are on a spiritual path, you recognise (or are open to) the deeper significance of your career. To you, your work is more than just a job which pays the bills. You have a yearning to understand your whole reason for being here on this earth in human form. You are searching for the connection between your earthly work and the spiritual realm and the more profound sense of mission which comes from that.

If you remember the Triple Purpose triangle, there is a direct line between your Higher Purpose and your Career Purpose. This connection between the two types of purpose can be experienced in a number of ways.

The Universe is working through you

The Universe needs you to carry out its own mission in human form. To express itself *through* you, through your creativity, your healing power, your support of others, your leadership and other gifts. Just as with your Life Purpose, when you recognise your true spiritual nature, you open up as a channel for the Universal Life Force energy to flow through you and activate your Career Purpose.

When you are doing the work which the Universe has sent you to do, it will also empower you to do so. When you connect to this energy stream (and get your Ego Self out of the way), you become more effective in your work. You realise that it isn't really you who is doing it, or at least not you alone. You are working in collaboration with the Universe. You connect to the Source. You let go of the imposter syndrome which has kept you stuck. You stop asking 'who do I think I am to do this work' and you ask the Universe 'how can I be of service'.

The Universe has chosen you

Even when you are on a spiritual path, you can still feel undeserving of this deeper mission and the idea that you have been selected for it. Recognise this as simply your Ego Self. I had a client who, because of his upbringing – on a council estate and in and out of social care – thought himself less deserving of carrying out this higher mission than others, despite having a real sense of the impact he could make in the world through his work.

Your current circumstances, your family background, your career history, your current skills, your current financial state do not matter. In fact, the Universe may have chosen you *because* of those things. Because it will give you a deeper understanding of the people you may be here to serve or a deeper feeling of joy and gratitude when you turn your circumstances around. Plus, through this Career Alignment Journey you will be given the opportunity to evolve, to learn new skills, to expand.

The Universe is guiding you

The fact that you are reading this book and perhaps feeling unsettled in your work may be the Universe pushing you away from something. Perhaps you sense a stirring from within your heart centre. Or an inner knowing that there is something else you are meant to be doing instead of what you are currently doing.

The Universe is always communicating with you. The question is, are you listening? Sometimes the messages are loud and clear and can whack you around the face. I certainly experienced this when I had my career-defining epiphany on a Norfolk beach back in 2015. Other times, the messages are delivered as faint little whispers which can easily get lost amidst any other noise. And even no clear communication at all can have a message in it, such as keeping us in a suspended state whilst other things are being lined up.

Your Career Purpose already exists. This doesn't mean that the next step you take has to be perfectly obvious right now or what you ultimately end up doing. It took me three separate career moves before I went from the corporate world to life as a coach. Each one was a 'step towards' which I felt guided to take. Just keep listening and noticing. The Universe is on this journey with you and is providing you with the information you need to live out your Career Purpose.

How to align with your Career Purpose in your current job

It is possible that you could find a way to connect with more purpose in your *current* job. Even in seemingly the most mundane of jobs lies the potential for greater purpose to be found. In some cases with clients, this has even negated the need to make a career change at all when they finally realised the opportunity which already existed.

I recommend you at least explore this idea. Even if you still intend to move into something new, it will enable you to put out a positive signal to the Universe around your intention. And create a higher vibration from which your new work circumstances can emerge.

The rest of this book is designed to enable you to evaluate whether you can find more purpose in your current work or whether you need to make a career change (and what that might look like). But in the meantime, here are some more immediate ways to bring a sense of purpose to your work.

Remind yourself who you are serving

When you are in a job where you feel unhappy, unfulfilled or undervalued, it can be easy to lose sight of the purpose of your role and feel disconnected from the people you are there to serve. Most jobs have an end customer of some description – be that clients, patients, students, colleagues or even animals and nature.

My Dad used to work as an accountant for a security alarm manufacturer. He was asked by a performance coach who had been hired by the CEO what his purpose was, to which he responded "to produce financial reports and balance the books." He was asked to reconsider his response and acknowledge how his work was in fact ultimately helping people feel safer and sleep easier in their beds at night. Although he loved his job anyway, realising this added an extra dimension and an even deeper sense of purpose to his work.

And then there is the classic story of when President Kennedy visited the NASA Space Centre back in 1962 and asked the janitor there what he did. His response was "I'm helping put a man on the moon, Mr President". This guy recognised his contribution to the team and how his job formed part of the bigger picture. It seems he understood the deeper sense of purpose which could be derived through his work.

What is the purpose of your employer? What is their 'why'? Is this something which you can connect with more or derive a more conscious level of fulfilment from?

Change the 'how'

Even if you aren't able to change *what* you are doing in your current job, you can at least change *how you do it*. This means that, as with your Life Purpose, you act as a vessel for love by simply changing your thoughts and your intention to bring more joy, more kindness and more light to others. And you practice acceptance of being where you are right now, whilst you figure out what else you want to do. This approach can be brought to any and every job, whether you're a cleaner, a teacher or a brain surgeon. Consider the places which might need it the most such as toxic corporate environments.

Whenever I visit my dentist, I am always struck by the joy and the lightness she brings to her practice. It's a rare thing to say about seeing a dentist, but I actually enjoy going! Previously, I would leave my appointments feeling diminished, often having picked up on quite a low vibration. When I switched practices, no longer prepared to experience this energy, it was like a huge breath of fresh air. It really took me aback. Here were two highly qualified professionals doing exactly the same job, but in totally different ways.

How you show up to your work is everything. The opportunity is there every day for you, even if ultimately you intend to do something different. How do you currently show up to your work, your clients, your colleagues? In what way might you be able to act as that vessel of love and light a little more?

Give yourself permission

If you are able to acknowledge the greater fulfilment potential within your current job, and that you don't need anything else right now to bring more connection to your purpose, it then comes down to giving yourself permission. Permission to act as that vessel and to show up to your job in a new way.

Often, the Ego Self will rear its head to say, "Who do you think you are to try and play." Or "You're not ready, you need to be more qualified or more enlightened first." It will attempt to make you feel undeserving or unworthy of being in that position.

I had a client who worked in a senior role in the energy sector in the Middle East. Through our sessions, it was clear that he already had a strong connection to his purpose. He had the support of his managers and a free rein to shape the role how he wanted and be a true ambassador within an area which he was passionate about. But imposter syndrome was holding him back and limiting his power and effectiveness in the role. Once he gave himself the permission to act out his purpose within his role and to evolve with it, he started making an even more meaningful contribution to his organisation and began realising more of his true potential.

The Purpose Tree: A nature-inspired model for aligning with your Career Purpose

I love the symbolism of nature. There is so much we can draw from it both to guide and inspire us in our daily life and to help us see the bigger picture and how cyclical things are. In particular, I have always felt very connected to trees and, during my many dog walks over the years, I have always sensed they would one day serve as an important metaphor within my work in some way.

And so, drawing inspiration from the tree, I created a model to help define my own approach and philosophy behind making a career change and aligning with purpose. It has supported many of my clients through their career changes and will also form the basis of Part 3 of this book.

The guiding principle behind this approach is that in the same way that for a tree to flourish it must have strong roots, for you to flourish in your working life, you too must have strong foundations in place.

Some approaches to career change focus more heavily on the outer aspects such as researching the job market, updating a CV and making new connections. All in the hopes that it might just be a better fit this time, but without ever getting to the heart of the matter or understanding what truly makes a person tick. This invariably leads to repeating the same career patterns. It is like sticking a plaster on a wound without ever properly allowing it to heal. This was my experience until I noticed the pattern and journeyed within.

The approach we will be taking works from the ground up by setting your foundations first so that your career is then the outer manifestation of what is going on inside. It sees you as a whole being, not just a person who does a job, in isolation from the rest of your life experience.

To explain this approach, we will briefly explore the three main elements of the tree (the roots, the trunk and the leaves/fruit), each of which represents the three different states of our existence: Being, Doing and Having.

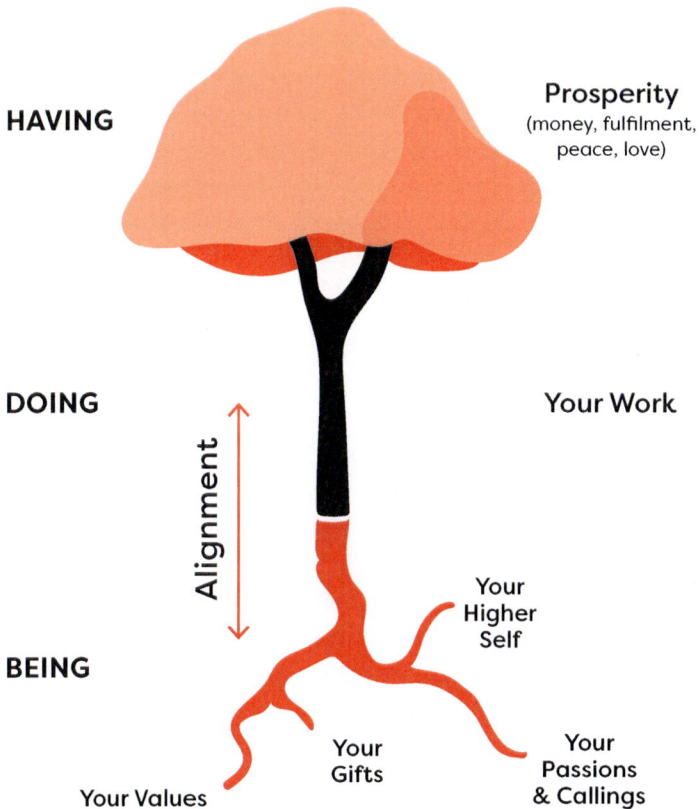

HAVING

Prosperity
(money, fulfilment, peace, love)

DOING

Your Work

Alignment

BEING

Your Higher Self

Your Gifts

Your Passions & Callings

Your Values

BEING: The roots (the essence of who you are)

Your 'Being' is the essence of who you are – both on a human and a spiritual level. It is the part of you which is mostly hidden from view but from which all the outer aspects of your working life – what you do and what you have (the trunk and leaves of the tree) stem.

Through this process, the aim first and foremost is to gain fresh clarity on who you truly are within and on what is truly important to you at your core. To reveal or reconnect with those parts of you which may have gotten lost over the years, perhaps as a result of the work environment you have been in, or the responsibilities or challenges of life which have obscured them from your view.

There are four major 'roots' which form part of your Being in the context of this model. Gaining clarity on these four roots will enable you to make a profound and lasting career change.

We will look at each of them in detail over the next four chapters.

- Your Higher Self
- Your Values
- Your Passions and Callings
- Your Gifts

If you focus on your Doing without first focusing on your Being, your foundation is likely to be shaky. And that can lead to making career decisions which aren't fully aligned with who you truly are. Or attempting to find career alignment by grasping which is less conducive to attracting what you want. This is why I always recommend starting with Being.

DOING: The trunk (your work)

Your 'Doing' is the work which you do. For the most part, once you have full clarity on your Being, your Doing will emerge organically – just as the trunk will emerge from the roots. Similarly, your alignment with your Career Purpose is, in a sense, a natural process. And when you have firm roots in place, just like the tree, you will have a stronger trunk. Your work will be more potent and empowered and you will make a greater impact in the world.

Often, once they have gained clarity on their Being, a client can have a 'lightbulb moment' on what their new career path (their Doing) is. What was once confusing for them suddenly becomes so natural, so obvious. The fog begins to lift.

It is important to note that while the answer will be obvious for some as to what their aligned career path is, for others it may take a little more time to unravel and clarify. There is no 'right' or 'wrong'. I encourage you to trust in your path and how clear things are when you get to that stage. And to listen closely to the guidance and the intuitive nudges you receive about your Doing and what feels in alignment for you.

To help you with this on a more practical level, in Chapters 12 and 13 we will explore various career path options and drill down into the specifics of a new job, a new employer and a new sector so that you can see how the four roots can be brought to life.

Another aspect of your Career Purpose 'unravelling' is acknowledging those things which might be blocking you from aligning with it such as any limiting beliefs or ego-based patterns which have held you back or kept you stuck. You may want to revisit Chapter 4 to help you with that if and when any blocks arise.

HAVING: The leaves and fruit (your prosperity)

Your 'Having' is the outer benefits of your career – your prosperity. This includes the money that you earn. Money is likely necessary to make your Career Purpose sustainable. Whilst you are doing your purposeful work, you need to be able to live and to support yourself and possibly also your family.

However, I also want to offer you a broader definition of prosperity. It is a definition which includes other things such as peace, joy, love, fulfilment and wellbeing and which takes your potential career change into a higher realm. It allows you to be guided by something much deeper and much more profound than a purely financial incentive alone.

And, just as a tree will produce more abundant fruit or leaves from a strong and healthy trunk and deep, firm roots, so too will you enjoy more prosperity from doing work which is alignment with your Being. This is a law of nature. You become part of the natural flow of abundance.

The Purpose Tree demonstrates how you can enjoy both career fulfilment and prosperity rather than an either/or scenario which many people believe will be the case when looking to make a career change. The 1987 classic book *Do What You Love, The Money Will Follow*[10] by Marsha Sinetar points towards this truth.

When your work is in alignment with who you truly are and you are serving the world by living out your purpose, money will flow to you. You are in a higher vibration where you attract prosperity to you. You are trusting in the flow.

I believe that we all deserve to live in abundance and that money is a symbol of our connectedness with Source. It is also a vehicle for us to be able to experience the fullness of life – be that in the form of nourishing ourselves, having new experiences, travelling the world, living in beautiful surroundings which put us in a higher vibration state or being able to give to other people.

Money is also an important consideration because of how it can trigger you and sometimes make you question your own worth. Again, it is an essential part of this process to explore these triggers and transcend any possible blocks or resistance to you opening up to your own abundance.

CHAPTER HIGHLIGHTS

- Your Career Purpose is to make a difference in the world by doing the work you are called to do, using the gifts you have been given.

- Your Career Purpose already exists – it is more about aligning with it internally rather than trying to look for it externally.

- Aligning with your Career Purpose can transform your life in many ways such as bringing you a new-found inner confidence, improving your relationships and your wellbeing.

- There are many ways you can align more with your Career Purpose in your current job, such as changing 'how' you do your job.

- The Purpose Tree is a nature-inspired approach to aligning with your Career Purpose and highlights the importance of beginning with your roots.

Journalling questions

How motivated are you to align with your Career Purpose? What specifically is motivating you?

What action can you take to bring a little more purpose to your current job?

In what ways can you show up to your work in a more purposeful or impactful way and act as a channel for the Universe to work through?

What approach have you taken to any previous attempts to find more purpose in your career? Did you start with Having, Doing or Being?

What aspects of prosperity are most important to you and will motivate you to make a more profound career change?

PART 3:
PLANTING YOUR ROOTS

When you operate from the Higher Self, you feel centred and abundant, in fact, overflowing. When you experience this abundance, your fears automatically disappear.

SUSAN JEFFERS

CHAPTER 8:
Root #1 – Your Higher Self

The first of the four roots is your Higher Self. Your Higher Self is the essence of who you are on a spiritual level. It is the non-physical dimension of your Being. It is the wise, loving, authentic, unlimited and eternal part of you. It is the source of Universal light and love which resides within you. It is the 'being' part of 'human being'. And it just so happens that it is also where your true potential for a *quantum leap* within your career lies.

Your Higher Self is always with you and available to you, either in the background or in a more obvious way such as when you meditate. It cannot be experienced intellectually or by the rational mind. It is experienced as a state of consciousness, an inner connection, an inner knowing.

The Higher Self is the self which is separate from your Ego Self. It is the part of you which transcends your limiting beliefs, fears and worries. The body, your human form, is the vehicle which houses the Higher Self.

I believe that in understanding and harnessing your Higher Self, the work you do on aligning your career becomes more deep and meaningful. And that the challenge of your current career situation can actually serve as a helpful catalyst for you to awaken to this deeper aspect of yourself which, in turn, can support you in all other areas of your life.

Whether you already have awareness of your Higher Self or this is the first time you have ever explored the concept, I invite you to trust in what has led you to be reading these words and where this part of the journey can take you.

Characteristics of the Higher Self

To understand exactly what the Higher Self is, it can be helpful to identify some of its characteristics, just as we did with the Ego Self.

Identifies with
Inner intangible things (spirit, soul, essence)

How it feels in the body
Light, expansive, free, open

Focuses on
The present moment
Being authentic
The bigger picture
Growth

Words and phrases
You/we/ours, I choose, I trust

Likes
Surrender, humility, being true

Skills
Listening

Accepting
Trusting
Intuiting
Letting go
Sharing

Beliefs
There is plenty to go around (abundance)
My own truth is what really matters
I am innately worthy

Driven by
Collaboration and compassion

Consequences
Inner peace, calm, balance

Born out of
Love

At the root of all of these Higher Self characteristics is *love*. Love is the guiding force which underpins any actions which come from your Higher Self. A quick way to sense check whether you are acting from your Higher Self is to ask whether your thoughts or actions are rooted in *love* (as opposed to *fear* when they are coming from the Ego Self).

How your Higher Self will support you

I often wonder how my career might have turned out had I not called on my Higher Self at various points along my journey. It is hard to put into words exactly how it has supported me. I think the best analogy is perhaps that of a GPS navigation system working in the background, enabling me to constantly course correct on my path towards my true purpose.

My Higher Self has provided me with a sort of 'ledge' on which I have been able to stand at times to rise above my human experience, to see the bigger picture, to take more of a witness stance and to make sense of things, especially when they didn't quite turn out as I had planned.

And, perhaps most significantly, connection to my Higher Self has enabled me to take not one but three leaps of faith by leaving jobs which were out of alignment with nothing else to go into.

Here are some of the ways in which your Higher Self can support you on your Career Alignment Journey.

1. Self-worth

Having a solid foundation of self-worth is perhaps the most profoundly important reason for accessing the Higher Self. Your self-worth is the value or importance you place on yourself. Low self-worth can have a debilitating impact on your Career Alignment Journey. Perhaps it has already.

Low self-worth can be the product of many different things. And they are all human in form and origin. For example, how you were treated as a child, perhaps if you had overly-critical or neglectful parents, can massively impact your self-worth and the opinion you have of yourself as an adult. However, I do know that on a *spiritual* level, there is salvation to be found from low self-worth through the Higher Self. And this can be the difference-maker.

The Higher Self knows that you are a Divine Being and are therefore *innately* worthy. You are an expression of the Universe, of God, of the Divine. You are equally as worthy as anyone and everyone else. In this way the spiritual realm provides a level playing field. So, no matter what your past or current circumstances on a human level, you have a source of deep self-worth you can access through the Higher Self.

2. Clarity and guidance

The need for clarity is the number one reason why clients come to career coaching. Many report initially feeling lost and confused and unable to see the wood for the trees. Connection to the Higher Self brings clarity. It brings a connection with the source of truth and inner knowing. There are no filters, no fears, no barriers. The Higher Self knows what is for your highest good and will guide you towards it.

The lightbulb moment I experienced on the Norfolk beach which led me to becoming a coach was a message which I believe was given to me as a result of me connecting with my Higher Self. For me, the sea provides a clear point of connection with the Universe and a means with which to tune into my Higher Self. I asked for an answer on what to do next in my career and received a very clear response which I felt with every fibre of my being in that moment.

It can be a huge comfort, knowing that you don't have to figure it all out on your own. The key is to listen out for the guidance and to be open to the signs and signals which the Universe presents to you through your Higher Self.

I do also want to acknowledge here, though, that sometimes the guidance is not always what it first seems. Occasionally, the Universe doesn't bring us quite what we had asked for but it does so with the bigger picture and ultimately your growth in mind. As Gabrielle Bernstein puts it, "Sometimes your higher self will guide you to make mistakes so you can learn lessons".

3. Confidence and courage

When I first started out as a coach, I used to worry about what people would think of me when I started 'putting myself out there'. For example, sharing my thoughts and ideas on social media, using my name for my business and having photos of myself on my website. I would not have written this book had I not called on my Higher Self to help me overcome these worries and tap into a deeper source of confidence and courage.

Because I feel so guided in what I do, and I recognise that it's not about me (it's about the people I am here to help), I have total conviction in what I am doing – the likes of which I have never experienced before. I acknowledge that all of those worries and concerns were coming from my Ego Self. The 'little me' who was making choices based on fear instead of love.

That's not to say that everyone will love what I do! I know that what I share will not resonate with some people. I am OK with that. I know that I am not for everyone. But the point I am trying to make is that I am not letting the fears around not being for everyone stop me anymore.

When you call on your Higher Self and you trust in your path, it brings you a certain sense of security, a sure-footedness. Leaving a job which brings you a regular wage takes courage. Setting up a new business with no guarantee of clients and income takes courage. Working within a new sector or even just a new employer can take courage. But when you do these things in connection with your Higher Self, you know that you cannot 'fail'. You always have a safe harbour to come home to every day. You trust in the bigger picture and why things have happened the way they have. You trust that it will be leading you to exactly where you need to be.

4. Fresh perspective

Your Higher Self sees things from a different perspective to your earthly Ego Self. This can be a real comfort if you are experiencing some trying circumstances in your life or your career right now. From this alternative, higher perspective, it is possible to have an alternative, higher response. To meet your challenges with a new energy, knowing that this is part of a bigger picture. It may be difficult to see what that bigger picture is right now, but your Higher Self trusts in the unfolding of your life plan. You become more patient on your journey instead of grasping and trying to control things which are ultimately out of your control.

I had a client who was experiencing a lot of difficulty with her ex-husband and the trauma she suffered in that relationship. It was getting in the way of her journey towards realigning her career to become a coach. After she took the time to connect with her Higher Self, she realised how this trauma and the ability to confront and release it was all part of her purpose here on earth. She realised how she was, in fact, being guided into transmuting her own experience in order to help other women in similar situations.

Also, it can be frustrating when it seems like you are doing all the work and yet nothing is happening. Sometimes the Universe can keep you in a 'holding pattern' whilst the right circumstances, people or resources are being lined up for you in the background. Your Higher Self understands this which then allows you to rest a little easier, knowing that everything is happening at just the right time.

5. Creativity and inspiration

When you connect with your Higher Self, you also access a source of creative power – the Universal Life Force energy. This creative power can support you by way of coming up with new ideas and inspiration for a more aligned career. It can also support you in the actual work that you do, enabling you to become more potent and effective.

I use a broader definition of the word 'creativity' which extends beyond the classical definition, referring to painting, drawing or crafting. Creativity is about bringing something into being which once didn't exist. My own definition encompasses a whole range of tangible creations such as this book, my website, the workbooks I use, the content I share on social media. It also encompasses intangible creations such as solutions and ideas for my business or my clients.

Opening your channels to get into the creative flow can make you more effective in, for example, your writing, your generation of ideas, your ability to solve problems or your plans to set up your own business.

Creativity and inspiration go hand in hand. The word 'inspired' is derived from the words 'in' and 'spirit'. By living in connection to your spirit, via your Higher Self, you are living in connection with the source of inspiration. This is a valuable currency on your Career Alignment Journey and in any job that you do.

6. Inner peace and calm

The Career Alignment Journey can be a rollercoaster of emotions and can spark feelings of turmoil and resistance. Your Higher Self provides an inner sanctuary from the outside world. It offers a way to cut through the incessant noise of anxious thoughts, challenging people or circumstances and connect you with feelings of deep peace and calm.

When you respond to things from your Higher Self, there is more acceptance rather than resistance to what is. The higher vibration states of peace and acceptance will align you energetically with the new working life you are seeking. Accessing inner peace and calm will not only enable you to enjoy the alignment journey a whole lot more, it will give you something valuable to bring to others. It is a state of being which can be felt in the workplace – in meetings, challenging situations or interactions with colleagues or customers.

Intuition: The voice of your Higher Self

Your Higher Self communicates with you through your intuition. The Cambridge Dictionary defines intuition as 'an ability to understand or know something immediately based on your feelings rather than facts'[11].

I like to think of intuition as a built-in guidance system which we all have at our disposal. A system which can help us make decisions which are for our highest good and often with far greater ease than figuring things out on a purely cognitive or fact-based level. Listening to your intuition can save a lot of time and stress on your Career Alignment Journey and provide a shortcut to realising your purpose and potential.

How your intuition communicates with you

Your intuition can communicate with you in a number of different ways, such as:

- Feeling excited or uneasy in your stomach (a 'gut feeling' about someone or something).

- Being 'pulled' towards something or someone, often with no obvious sense of why.

- Receiving messages and thoughts which seem to have come out of nowhere (a 'lightbulb moment').

- Recurring desires or nagging thoughts which don't seem to leave you.

- A sense in your body that something just 'feels right'.

- A faint whisper in the background.

It can also help you to detect your intuition by separating what appears to have come from your head versus your heart. Something which you sense is coming from the head is often more of a cognitive thought whereas something which is more of a feeling coming from the heart is likely to be your intuition.

Overcoming overthinking

Over time, as humans we have become increasingly disconnected from our intuition and often attempt to figure things out purely through logic and the thinking mind. When you constantly try and process the same thing in your mind, you start overthinking. Overthinking is a very common and debilitating habit I observe in my clients when they first come to coaching. Somewhere in there is an ingrained belief that the answers can be found through continuous thought.

However, once you start to listen to, trust and act on your own inner wisdom, your life can flow with much greater ease, and you will begin aligning with the people and opportunities which are for your highest good. This is incredibly helpful on your Career Alignment Journey. When you tap into this inner knowing you can access a new level of guidance on which path to take. Here are some of the ways in which intuition has supported my clients:

- Responding to an urge to call an old boss who then ended up sending them potential clients for their new business.

- Not accepting a job which didn't feel right, even though it looked good on paper.

- Being able to properly prioritise their values which helped to guide their decision making.

- Listening to the inner whisper that they were meant to be doing something else.

Acting on your intuition

Of course, *listening* to your intuition is only one part of the equation. The other part is *acting* on it. This is a lesson in trust. Your intuition is, in a sense, like a muscle. It needs to be used regularly to become strong and to support you. And, the more you listen and trust, the more guidance you will receive.

Your intuition won't always make complete sense at the time. Your Higher Self sees the bigger picture, which may take time to be revealed to you. Try not to judge the messages you receive through your intuition. Stay open to what they could be about and how they could be moving you towards your highest good.

To build the trust needed to act on your intuition more, it can help to reflect back on your life and identify any times when you have listened to your intuition and also any times when you have not. Can you recall a time when you had a clear message about something – maybe a job which you knew deep down wasn't right for you but which you took anyway? Or maybe an opportunity you had to explore a new interest which you felt drawn to but which you turned down through fear?

Seven ways to access your Higher Self

Now you have greater awareness of what the Higher Self is and how it can support you, here are some ways you can access and connect with it.

1. Strengthen your intuition

Start strengthening your intuitive muscle with this suggested practice.

- During the next seven days, become aware of when you have a *feeling* or a *sense* about something or someone. This could be related to your career or something entirely separate.

- For each day, make a note in your journal of what comes through for you. How did you experience that intuition? Was it a gut feeling, a thought which seemed to come from nowhere or maybe a feeling of excitement or being pulled towards something?

- Choose at least one intuitive feeling which you decide to act upon. This can be something small or simple to start with such as following a hunch to drive down a certain street where there might be a parking space. Or calling someone who you have been thinking of 'out of the blue'.

- Monitor and make a note of what happens with anything you

have chosen to act upon. This might go beyond the seven days. Consider any benefits of acting from your intuition versus logic. For example, did it save you any time or stress?

- Also note if you have any resistance to acting on that intuition.

2. Imagine your 30-year older self

This is a powerful exercise I use with many clients which can instantly enable them to access their Higher Self.

- Close your eyes (if it feels safe to do so) and imagine right now being in the shoes of your 30-year older self. Imagine the physical details of what you might look like – your hair, your clothing, and where you might be standing – on a beach, in your office, on a mountain.

- From that vantage point, imagine now that you are looking at your current self. Really look at yourself and again notice the details.

- What advice or message would you like to pass on to your current self in relation to what you are going through in your life or career right now?

- How does that feel? What emotions come up for you? How easy was it for you to give this message to your current self?

- Gently open your eyes, when you feel ready to do so, and then make a note of this message in your journal.

This is not in fact your *30-year older* self as you can only ever be your *current* self. This is actually your Higher Self which you have accessed. This is the part of you which knows the truth. The part of you which can give you a more loving, supportive response. And it is available to you at all times.

3. Pay attention to your dreams

Your Higher Self can also communicate to you through your dreams. When you are in the REM (rapid eye movement) stage of sleep, you become relaxed and receptive enough for the messages to come through.

- Set an intention before you fall asleep to meet your Higher Self in your dream that night.

- In the morning, as you awaken, recall the details of your dream and make a note in your journal and of any feelings or sensations which came up for you. You might find it helpful to keep your journal at the side of your bed.

- See if you can sense what message your Higher Self is trying to pass on to you.

- If it doesn't feel too clear, then ask for further guidance and stay aware of any recurring themes in your dreams.

4. Do some intuitive writing

You can also use your journalling practice, or begin one, to get in touch with your Higher Self by asking some direct questions and letting the intuitive answers flow. Here are some suggested questions to ask your Higher Self as a starting point.

- What is my soul yearning for right now?

- What do you need me to know right now?

- What lessons am I being shown right now?

- What is my part in making this quantum leap?

- What is my purpose in this lifetime?

- What is just the next step I need to take?

Trust in what comes out onto the pages for you, even if it doesn't make total sense for you right now.

5. Become aware of your Ego Self

One of the simplest ways of accessing your Higher Self is becoming aware of when you are operating out of the opposite – your Ego Self. This can act as a powerful trigger and reminder to call in the Higher Self. It is also the first step you need to take to *transcend* the Ego Self.

As an in-the-moment practice, simply notice these thoughts and feelings and recognise that you have a choice to call on your Higher Self for an alternative view or an alternative response or way of handling things. You might find it helpful to cross reference the individual characteristics of the Higher Self versus the Ego Self.

6. Meditate

There are many guided meditations available online to enable you to meet your Higher Self. However, I recommend a simple unguided meditation as a starting point. The essence of meditation is about quieting your mind and going within. It provides an ideal access point for you to connect with your Higher Self.

You can use the meditation guidance in Chapter 3 to start your meditation practice, and then add these steps.

- Begin by setting an intention to connect with your Higher Self during your meditation.

- Imagine the most loving, peaceful, expansive version of

yourself as a presence either just above and around your head or emanating from your heart centre.

- See if you notice any sensations which might indicate that you have connected with your Higher Self, such as a feeling of warmth, a sense of spaciousness, a calm loving energy or a higher vibration.

- Consider what emotions you feel once you are connected with your Higher Self – do you feel more free, more trusting, more secure, more abundant?

7. Use an affirmation

Try adding a simple affirmation into your Daily Spiritual Practice which connects you with your Higher Self, such as:

- I open to listening out for and receiving intuitive guidance.

- Today, I choose to act more from my Higher Self.

- The answers I seek are already within me.

- I trust in my Higher Self to guide and support me on my journey.

- When I connect with my Higher Self, I connect with my true power.

You may prefer to create one of your own. Either way, I recommend repeating your chosen affirmation at least three times during each session. And work with your affirmation for 30 days so that it fully integrates into your consciousness.

CHAPTER HIGHLIGHTS

- Your Higher Self is the essence of who you are on a spiritual level and is always available to you.

- Your current career challenge can serve as a catalyst to awaken you to your Higher Self which will also positively impact all other areas of your life.

- Calling on your Higher Self will support you on your Career Alignment Journey.

- Your Higher Self communicates to you through your intuition.

- You can overcome the debilitating impact of overthinking by listening to your inner wisdom.

Journalling questions

How might your Higher Self support you on your Career Alignment Journey?

How often do you listen to or notice any intuitive thoughts or feelings?

How does your intuition typically come through for you, for example, a faint whisper, a gut feeling, a sense of something feeling 'right'?

What intuitive thoughts or feelings have you maybe had about which career path to take (or not take)?

Which activity will you commit to trying to help you access your Higher Self?

*It's not hard
to make decisions
when you know
what your
values are.*

ROY E DISNEY

CHAPTER 9:
Root #2 – Your Values

If I could only take one coaching exercise with me to a desert island, this would be it. Clarifying and prioritising your values is fundamental to creating alignment across all areas of life. Your values pervade your work, your relationships, your wellbeing, and your sense of fulfilment. And they are a critical part of the root system which will enable you to realign your career. If you want to create a deep and lasting change in your career, or your life, then your values must come into play.

In a sense, your values are like the operating system on which you are running your life. And, just like when your computer or mobile phone starts to malfunction or slow down because of an outdated operating system, so too can you when you are aligned with an outdated set of values. So, it's time now to take a fresh look at your values so that you can re-boot and upgrade your operating system.

What is a value?

A value is something intangible which you place importance on within your life. It represents a source of deep motivation and an outer expression of your authentic self.

The word 'intangible' is important here to decipher whether something is a value or not. A simple illustration of this is money. Money, as something tangible, would not be a value. However, what money brings you such as financial security, which is intangible, would be the underlying value.

Whilst some of your values may remain static, many of them will change over time. What was important to you in your twenties may well be different to what is important to you in your thirties and your forties and so on.

Adventure was far more important to me in my twenties and thirties which is one of the reasons why I spent time in different countries and appreciated an element of travel within my previous career. I also highly valued social connection and stimulation which is why I chose to live and work in London.

Now, I place much more value on inner peace, purpose and freedom. Clarifying these has given me a daily reminder of how much I am in alignment (something which I include in my daily gratitude practice).

Living out of alignment with your values

When you live out of alignment with your values, it can manifest as feeling deeply unfulfilled, uneasy, restless, disconnected and even depressed. You can become frustrated, lost and swept along by the current with nothing to anchor you.

If you were drawn to reading this book, it is possible that your career is still aligned to an old, outdated set of values that were once important to you but no longer are (or at least some of them). If so, it's time to wipe the slate clean and start afresh.

During my final couple of years in the corporate world, I felt like what can only be described as 'a round peg in a square hole'. I just didn't seem to see the world in the same way as many other people who worked there saw it, nor did I resonate with the philosophy of the organisation or the industry I worked in.

When I look back now, I can see quite clearly that some of my core values were not being honoured in that environment. And it affected me. Deeply. I sometimes wish I had done this work on my values back in those days because everything would have made more sense to me. And then I realise that this is exactly what I was meant to experience at that time.

The signs of misalignment in your working life

There are many situations within your working life which could indicate that you are out of alignment with your values. Here are some of the ones which crop up quite often in my coaching sessions. See if you can recognise yourself in any of them.

- Following a career path or doing a job which is more important to someone else, such as a parent, than it is to you.

- Hanging onto a job just because you think you 'should'.

- Feeling detached or disconnected from your industry, your organisation or your colleagues.

- Feeling continuously stressed or experiencing burnout.

- Lacking any other focus or interest outside of your job.

- Keeping parts of yourself under wraps at work, for example, your creative or spiritual side.

- Feeling like your heart isn't in it with the work you do.

- Going along with things which don't sit well with you such as discussions in team meetings or your company's strategy.

How acknowledging your values will help you

I have been working with clients on defining their values for many years and I have always found the exercise to have an impact. This impact has sometimes been subtle but it also been life-changing.

Fresh clarity on your career path

Acknowledging your values brings you a deeper understanding of why you feel so misaligned in your current work situation. Rather than it just being a general sense of malaise, you can pinpoint the specific values which are not being honoured, such as autonomy or trust. Your values help you to clarify the elements you need in your working life in order to feel happier and more fulfilled and how. This can then help in making a choice as to whether to stay in your current role or leave it for something new.

For example, if the values of freedom and creativity rank highly you may then have a leaning towards self-employment. Or if you highly prize human connection and making a difference you may start to open your mind towards a career in a helping profession.

More motivation to take action

To convert your intentions and goals into action, motivation is required. Motivation will stop you from just ambling along and instead grasp the nettle and get moving with things. If you go about the exercise of uncovering your values (which follows shortly) in an intuitive way and really listen within to how they make you feel, they will provide a deep source of motivation.

As inner peace is one of my top values, it gives me the motivation every day to do my spiritual practice of yoga and meditation. I know how much this will help me to feel aligned and so I am much more willing to invest the time each morning. Similarly, clients who are motivated by the value of health or wellbeing then become much more motivated to take action in putting firmer boundaries in place or looking for a role which affords them better balance.

Living more authentically

When you are living in alignment with your values, you are living from your own true essence. You have a deeper sense of inner connection. It just feels right. You start to acknowledge what is important to you instead of applying some enforced rules or society's view of what is most important. This is the authentic you. And it deserves to be honoured.

For years I was swept along in the corporate world where the main aim was making profit and selling lots of products to lots of people. I often wondered why I didn't have the same drive and determination to succeed or even the same passion for products that some of my colleagues had. I realise now that I wasn't living from my own essence. I was being inauthentic. I was not honouring some of my core values. How I feel about my work now is entirely different. And it turns out that the drive and determination I saw in others was there in me all along. I was just in the wrong job.

Making more conscious choices

When you stay aware of your values, they can become a set of guiding principles which support you in your decision making and help keep you on course with any choices you make. Whether these are simple daily choices, such as making time in your day for some creativity, or bigger, life-changing ones, such as whether to leave your long-standing career of twenty years. Your values will help you navigate your course more smoothly and more efficiently.

However, it is important to give yourself regular reminders of your values so they stay in your awareness. As another 'in-the-moment' practice, I also recommend that when you need to make a choice or decision, take a little pause beforehand. You can then bring your values to mind and sense whether or not this is an aligned choice or decision.

Clarifying your top ten values

For this exercise on clarifying your values, I am not going to ask you to sit and list all your values out. Nor am I about to give you a list of values to choose from. Instead, we will use a much more organic approach through a set of specific questions designed to elicit them from you naturally. To get the most out of this exercise, I recommend that you:

- Set aside some quality time and head space. Your values inform every part of your life, so it is worth the investment.

- Answer as intuitively as you can. Try not to overthink this exercise or second guess yourself with what you come up with. Listen from your heart and your soul for the answers and trust in yourself.

- Don't judge yourself for what comes up.

- Be sure not to include any values which you think 'should' be on your list or any which may be influenced by others – be that your partner, your parents, your friends or society generally.

- Allow full clarity on your values to emerge. Come back to the exercise over the course of at least a week and go for some mindful walks to meditate on it.

- Once complete, keep your top ten list of values out where you will see it on a daily basis rather than putting it in a drawer or keeping it on your computer. It will provide an anchor for you and help you stay on course at key moments when you might be heading out of alignment or feeling off balance.

Download your free Values Worksheet in the Book Resources, which you can access through this link:

rebeccakirk.co.uk/book-resources

Step 1. Brainstorm your values

The first step in this exercise is to brainstorm your values. I will now guide you through some topics and questions, firstly within the area of your work and then within the area of your life. The reason we will look at both is so that you can create more balance and wholeness than from a list purely focused on your work values. However, you can do this exercise separately for your work values and for your life values if that feels like it makes more sense to you. Grab your journal and let's see what comes up for you.

Work-related values

Q1. What first drew you to your current or last job?

When you are feeling desperate to leave your job, it can be easy to lose sight of what first drew to it. But there may be a few clues within those reasons as to what some of your values are.

In considering the question above, try breaking it down into the following:

- What first drew you to the industry/sector?

- What first drew you to the employer (or to self-employment)?

- What first drew you to the role?

Here are some examples of the types of things which may have drawn you in and the potential *value* lying underneath:

- **The people** - was this because you value human connection?

- **The money** - was this to bring you a sense of security?

- **The location** - was this to enable you to have better work life balance?

- **The role** - did this offer you an opportunity to learn and grow?

- **The company** - did this perhaps bring you a certain status?

Which of these values are still important to you? Of course, some may no longer be compelling for you. Only keep on your brainstorm list those values which are *still* important to you.

I had a client who was working as a counsellor and was feeling quite lost and searching for new meaning in her career. When she reflected on her reasons for becoming a counsellor and how this highlighted two of her continuing values – making a difference and authentic relationships – she reconnected to her work.

You might feel the urge with some jobs to state that you 'just fell into it', rather than ever having had a feeling of being *drawn* to it. However, I would like to challenge you to still search for a possible reason as there may be some hidden values which were at play. For example, taking a flexible or short-term contract role meant that you could focus on other things, such as travelling and honour the value of freedom. Or perhaps you were driven by the need to simply earn some money at the time which brought you some security or enabled you to enjoy a certain lifestyle.

If getting into your current job was less of a considered or conscious choice, then this time represents an even greater watershed moment for you. Now is your opportunity to realign your career by bringing your values into the mix and making it a conscious choice.

I recommend now repeating this question with all of the jobs you have ever had.

Q2. What has kept you in your current job up until now?

Whilst you may have a strong urge to get out of your current work situation, it is also worth exploring what might have kept you there, up until this point. The answer to this question may be similar to your answer to question one, the money and the people for example. But it is nonetheless worth asking as it may reinforce what your values are or how many of them have endured over time. Perhaps you have wanted to see a certain project through to completion or, if you are a teacher, to complete a school year or term. This might indicate that loyalty or commitment is important to you.

Stay aware of any reasons for staying in your current job which are purely fear-based. For instance, fear of what your colleagues may think if you quit, fear of your family's reaction, or even fear of losing your house. Only keep the reasons (values) which come from a place of love rather than fear.

Q3. What are the positive stand-out moments of your career so far?

When you look back on your career, what specific moments, events or day-to-day happenings stand out to you? What things bring you a sense of satisfaction, happiness or achievement? These could seem like small or simple things, such as having made a positive impact on one customer or colleague. Or they could be on a bigger scale, such as delivering a challenging project which impacted a whole community. You might want to start with your current role and work backwards.

In one of my roles as a product manager, I was responsible for a multi-million pound range of products which were stocked in hundreds of shops. Whilst there was a level of satisfaction which came from that, my stand-out moments actually came from the small team I managed and from helping them to develop and feel valued and nurtured. Because of this, I knew deep inside that one day those things would become a more integral part of the work I did.

Q4. What is triggering you to want to change your work situation?

Often, the things which trigger you at work can provide clues around those values which are *not* being honoured. What aspects do you dislike about your current job, your current industry or your current working situation? Here are a few examples of things I have heard quite often from clients – alongside the value it demonstrated was lacking:

- An overbearing boss – lack of autonomy and trust

- An 'always on' culture where a response is expected 24/7 – lack of balance or wellbeing

- Demanding colleagues who never show gratitude – lack of appreciation or feeling valued

- A job or company with no prospects – lack of personal growth

- An organisation with a purely financial aim – lack of purpose or fulfilment

- Unrealistic targets – lack of understanding

- Work which is highly repetitive – lack of stimulation, challenge or variety

- Too much office politics and negativity – lack of harmony or sincerity

- A ruthless management team – lack of empathy or kindness

Q5. What are the negative stand-out moments in your career so far?

When you look back on your career, what events or day-to-day happenings stand out to you as perhaps having made you feel frustrated or unhappy? I do not recommend you dwelling on any of these for too long. Instead, use them as signs or signals as to what you need from your career to feel more aligned.

Some of the events which clients have recalled and the need it highlighted include:

- Being promised a pay-rise and then having it taken back (the need for integrity).

- Being thrown in at the deep end on a new project or role with no support (the need for support and collaboration).

- Being made redundant despite years of performing well (the need for loyalty).

Of course, some negative stand-out moments may point towards things outside of your values. They may highlight the need for you to make some changes such as learning a new skill or improving your time management to keep up with the pace.

Life-related values

Q1. What things are important to you outside of your work?

Assuming that work doesn't take up 100 percent of your time and head space (even though it may feel like it sometimes) there will be other things which are also important in your life. These can often be overlooked, especially when your work or your job search starts to consume you. This is your opportunity to take a little step back and take a broader view of things.

You might want to consider this question in the context of certain different areas of your life and see what emerges.

- Physical wellbeing
- Mental wellbeing
- Spiritual wellbeing
- Relationships
- Prosperity
- Personal growth
- Fun and leisure
- Home

Q2. What are the positive stand-out moments of your life so far?

What stand-out moments in your life can you recall? Any events or occasions when you perhaps felt happy, blessed, fulfilled or in the flow of life. Again, these can big deemed as big events such as the birth of a child, meeting your partner, moving to another country, going on a trip around the world or kick-starting a voluntary project. Or they may be of a smaller, simpler nature such as enjoying a sunrise on a beach, learning to play an instrument, spending time with your family and friends or with a pet.

I appreciate that this can sometimes be a challenging question. The cloud of your current situation may be weighing heavy over you and block out the lighter blue-sky moments of your life. If nothing emerges immediately, just give yourself a little time to reflect on this question and see what presents itself.

Q3. What are your 'must-haves' for a happy life?

Your 'must-haves' are those values which you already know you can't live without. Some of them may be so implicit that you don't consider them values. Things such as security, freedom, love, happiness, or peace. Or they may seem too lofty or unattainable right now. I do encourage you to at least throw them into the mix if they resonate with you.

I often work with creative people for whom creativity is so much a part of them that they don't think to include it as a value. Or people who are deeply connected to their families who sometimes overlook values such as love or connection. The fact that you are reading this book could imply that you are searching for greater purpose, meaning or fulfilment. If so, then put those on your brainstorm list too.

Extract the value

Now look back through your answers and make sure you have extracted the value. If you aren't sure, ask yourself what it is about that situation which was important to you or what underpins it. And similarly, for the things which upset or trigger you, what underlying value has perhaps not been honoured?

Ego-based values

Watch out for any values which may be coming from the Ego Self and are based in fear. These can significantly impact your energy if they are not honoured and may actually be detrimental to your search for purpose. For example, 'control' may be something you value and when you cannot control something it sends you into a spin. There are many things in life which are out of your control. This may in fact highlight a thought pattern which you would benefit from releasing or the opportunity of connecting more with your Higher Self so that you can build greater surrender and trust in yourself to handle whatever comes your way.

Step 2. Rank your values

The next step is to narrow your brainstorm list of values down to just ten and then place those values into ranking order. This is really the essence of the exercise as it forces you to make a choice between different values. Doing this will help you to re-prioritise and make more aligned choices in your life and create more focus on your Career Alignment Journey.

Ranking your values can be challenging. To help you with this step I recommend that you try not to overthink it but instead *sense* which ones are most important and which *feel* most motivating to you or stir you in some way.

Step 3. Assess your values

For each value in your top ten list, now consider how much your life and your career are in alignment with that value and give it an 'alignment score' from zero to ten (with ten being fully aligned and zero being not aligned at all). Write your score in the boxes next to the value in your worksheet. Next, consider these questions.

What do your alignment scores indicate to you about how good a fit your current (or most recent) career is?

What do your alignment scores indicate to you about how much you are honouring your values within your life?

What ideas or thoughts have emerged for you about some changes you could make or a new career which may be a better fit with your values? (Don't worry if nothing has emerged for you yet.)

Step 4. Realign with your values

Now that you have become aware of what your values are and assessed how much you are in alignment with them, the final step is about beginning to realign with them.

1. Take one inspired action

How might you be able to bring your life or career into closer alignment with one or more of your values *now*, before you make any potentially bigger changes? Over the next seven days, what is *one* small next step you can take to improve the alignment score on just one of your values? Perhaps start with the one with the lowest score. For example, if creativity was one of your top ten values and you gave it an alignment score of two within your life, then you could get out your sketch pad or your paints and set aside thirty minutes to reconnect with your love of art.

2. Meditate on your values

What would it be like for you to be fully aligned with your values in your life and career? I invite you to take a few moments now to meditate on it.

- Find a comfortable position and close your eyes, if it feels safe to do so.

- Take three deep inhales and exhales.

- Do a body scan to release any tension from your crown down to your toes.

- Imagine those values on your list being part of your day-to-day existence.

- Allow any thoughts to come without judging them and simply let them pass through.

- How does it feel to be in alignment? What colours, shapes, words or sensations come up for you?

- Allow yourself to enjoy this experience for as long as you choose.

- When you are ready, gently open your eyes and bring yourself back into the room.

- Make a note of any thoughts, feelings or shifts you experience after this meditation in your journal. What changes for you? How motivating is this to you?

3. *Visualise and raise your vibration*

Over the next thirty days, keep visualising your life and your career in closer alignment to your values. Connect with any feelings which emerged during meditation. Be conscious of how much head space you might be giving to your *current* reality and any misalignment. Remember that your vibration is very powerful in attracting the right circumstances and people into your life. You can create a higher vibration simply by feeling happy and excited about living in alignment with your values.

CHAPTER HIGHLIGHTS

- Clarifying and prioritising your values is fundamental to creating alignment across all areas of life.

- Your values represent a source of deep motivation and an outer expression of your authentic self.

- It is possible that your career is still aligned to an old set of values which now needs to be updated.

- Your values can be used as guiding principles in your decision making and to help keep you in alignment with any choices you make.

- It is important to identify and exclude any values which are fear-based.

A timeless lesson for a deeply fulfilling life is to discover your calling, that special work or consuming occupation that fully engages your special talents with your passions.

ROBIN S. SHARMA

CHAPTER 10:
Root #3 – Your Passions and Callings

Your Passions and Callings, which make up the third root of the Purpose Tree, are another source of deep motivation and connection and thereby an important aspect of your Career Alignment Journey. When you honour your passions, it brings you a sense of vitality and aliveness. And when you integrate one of your passions into your work, it connects you with a daily source of meaning and purpose which can transform your entire life.

We look at your passions and callings together because a calling is very often derived from those things which you are most passionate about. That is not to say that all of your passions need to become a calling. They can, however, bring you some further clues as to where you might want to take your work in order to have a deeper experience of fulfilment.

I also want to caveat this chapter with a word of caution. Do not attach yourself to the need to emerge from it with a perfectly clear picture of what your calling is. Sometimes (often), this work and discovering clarity on your purpose can take time. I invite you instead to see this chapter, and indeed this whole book, as a 'moving towards' and an 'opening up to' your deeper purpose.

Your passions

Before we go fully into the topic of passions, let us first clarify what they actually are so that it might be easier to recognise and acknowledge them.

Your passions are those things, either within or outside of your work, which you:

- Find exciting.

- Have a particular interest in.

- Have strong feelings towards.

- Feel genuine enthusiasm for.

- Feel compelled to pursue on some level.

You may already have a passion which you regularly make time and space for in your life. Maybe you had certain passions you pursued in the past but then other priorities have since taken over. Or you might have simply lost connection to a more recent passion.

For some people, their passions are obvious, and they can instantly reel off half a dozen things which really stir them and get them fired up. However, for others, it is not so obvious. Occasionally when I begin talking to a client about their passions, I can sense them recoil. It is as though they don't want to expose the reality that work has taken over their entire life. Or that they hold a belief that they 'should ' have more things which they are passionate about, especially in comparison to others.

If it is not immediately obvious what your passions are or if you are wondering if you even have any passions at all, I encourage you not to feel disheartened. It might be that work and life responsibilities are obscuring your passions and you simply need a reminder. It might be that you are comparing yourself to others or using a narrow definition of the word 'passion'. Or it could be that you are on the verge of discovering a new passion and that this book is here to guide you to it.

How to identify your passions

To highlight or tease out your passions, we will look at four different lines of questioning. As you consider these questions, I recommend that you look out for any common threads running through your answers.

1. Spare time

How you choose to spend the precious time you have when you are neither working nor carrying out any life responsibilities can indicate a passion. The word 'choose' is very significant here. It implies that you are *consciously* responding to a desire or a need to do something. There is no forcing, no sense of obligation.

Things you choose to do in your spare time could range from something simple, such as relaxing and switching off or spending time with friends or family through to something more considered, for example:

- Getting out into nature or the outdoors

- Visiting museums or historic sites

- Cooking or baking

- Playing an instrument

- Creative pursuits, such as painting, furniture restoring or crafting

- Reading a certain genre of book

- Travelling

- Gardening

- Voluntary work

For most of my adult life I have chosen to spend a good chunk of my spare time reading books about spirituality and personal growth. It wasn't until after I had my lightbulb moment in 2015 and I reflected on my life that I realised what a huge passion of mine this was and how this could actually become my new career. The clues were there all along.

Perhaps there are some things you love doing in your spare time which could serve as a clue towards your next career move which you maybe overlook? Or perhaps there are some things which you just haven't carved out the time for yet but are deeply yearning to. Such as those things which used to bring you joy or connection such as painting or playing the piano.

Of course, there is not always a direct link between your passion and your future career. You might not end up becoming an artist or a pianist. However, allowing even just a small amount of time for one of your passions can send out a positive signal to the Universe that it is important to you. And that will, in turn, raise your vibration and lead you further down the path towards alignment and fulfilment.

Spend a little time now contemplating the answer to these questions about your spare time:

How do you currently choose to spend your time after all your other life or work responsibilities are taken care of?

What do you long to have the time or head space for right now?

What passions have you felt connected to in the past which you would like to reconnect with now?

If money was no object, what would you spend your time doing?

2. Knowledge

Similarly, the topics that you have a keen interest in sharing or gaining knowledge in can also give you some strong clues about your purpose. Looking at your bookshelf is a good place to start here – notice if there are any particular themes which emerge. Are a lot of your books concerned with wellbeing, for instance, or the world of art? Do you love reading the biographies of people in certain fields, such as entrepreneurs or people who have overcome challenges? My bookshelf could easily be the personal growth section of my local bookstore!

Have you always fancied studying a particular subject or course? If you had all the time in the world and a huge savings pot, what might you choose to get a qualification in? Would you love to go back to university and get a degree in psychology? Or maybe a diploma in photography or counselling?

What subjects are you always talking about with friends and family? What topics do you feel you are in your element with when they arise? Do you long to have more connections with people who you can discuss certain areas of interest with? These can all give clues to uncover your passions.

I worked with a client who had recently left her successful

career as a fashion designer for a high street retailer in search of something more meaningful. After prompting her to take a look at her bookshelf, she had the realisation how passionate she was about nature, healing and nutrition. She also realised how she had become disconnected from her love of cooking as one of her favourite ways to spend her spare time. She had long since craved taking a course in naturopathic medicine but had dismissed it, considering it frivolous. But, after giving this particular desire for knowledge breathing space, alongside the other work she had done on her values and her Higher Self and trusting her intuition, she saw how this could become her new aligned career path.

Take some time now to explore your passions with these questions:

What topics do you love finding out about? What is your favourite area of knowledge?

What do you feel like you are in your element with when you discuss with others?

What might you choose to study if time and money weren't a factor?

3. Inspiration

There are also massive clues about your passions residing within the things which inspire you. As I mentioned previously, being inspired literally means 'in spirit' so this way of extracting your passions has a direct link to the higher realms.

Things which you draw inspiration from could include:

- A person you know, for example, a friend, a family member, a colleague.

- A person you know of, for example, an actor, a musician or a business founder.

- A group of people, for example, a sports team, those in a certain profession, such as nurses.

- A brand, for example, one which has strong sustainability values.

- An organisation, for example, a charity.

- A practice or philosophy, for example, a certain branch of yoga, meditation or spirituality.

- A natural object, for example, flowers, birds, mountains or a sunset.

- A manmade object, for example, a piece of art or something innovative.

When you feel inspired it can often be accompanied by a sense of losing yourself in that moment or of having your inner light turned on. You may have experienced this being out in nature and seeing a beautiful sunrise, or playing a piece of music which stirred you in some way. Perhaps you have gotten lost listening to a discussion on a podcast. If you stay conscious of those sensations in your body, you can more readily identify your sources of inspiration which can offer you insights into your passions and, ultimately, a more aligned career path.

Feeling inspired can also often lead you into taking spontaneous action which you might otherwise not have bothered to take. Perhaps you have a friend who has shown great courage and determination in extricating themselves from a difficult situation and have since turned their life around and set up their own business. This may have prompted you to pick up this book, or to look at options for leaving your job and setting your own business up too.

Maybe you had a grandparent, who you have always admired, who had a creative passion and inspired you to connect with your creative side too. Maybe you are inspired to buy from certain brands which display eco-friendly credentials or give something back to their local community.

I have always felt hugely inspired by people who have broken the mould in some way and have been unafraid to carve out their own niche, regardless of public opinion. One such person is the Icelandic musician Björk. At an influential age, my late teens, she opened up my mind to a more expansive and authentic definition of creativity. This inspired me up until my mid to late 40s, as I began to carve out my own niche within my career.

I am also constantly inspired by nature. I am fascinated by how it teaches us about the cycles of life and encourages us to trust in how things can transform with the seasons. I prioritise my practice of getting out into nature for a mindful walk and to help connect with the Universe. And, of course, trees have provided me with the inspiration which has formed the basis of this book.

The practice of Kundalini Yoga, along with my wonderful Kundalini Yoga teacher Kathryn McCusker, has been inspiring me since I discovered it in Sydney back in 2010. It is a practice I can very easily lose myself in and has also facilitated a quantum shift across all areas of my life.

The central theme running through these and many of my other sources of inspiration is transformation and expansion. These are now an integral part of my work as a coach.

Spend some time exploring your sources of inspiration with these questions.

Who or what is inspiring you right now?

What lights you up inside?

What are you able to lose yourself in, for example, a TV show, a creative pursuit, a discussion?

4. Causes

Your passions may come from an entirely different source. They might be connected to the causes or issues you see in the world which stir you, whether on a global scale or a smaller, more local scale.

A cause is something which you feel compelled to support, promote, defend or advocate in some way. Perhaps you see a lack in something which frustrates you. Or perhaps you feel drawn towards protecting a certain group of people or certain animals or aspects of nature.

Here are some examples of such causes:

- Giving more support to women suffering domestic abuse

- Better protection of our bee population

- Including life skills such as meditation in the school curriculum

- Doing business in a more conscious and compassionate way

- Reducing loneliness in the elderly

You may have found an outlet for a passion like one of those through voluntary work, giving to a particular charity, or even through your current job. There are many careers which stem from being passionate about a cause. Most obviously, those within the charity or NGO (non-governmental organisation) sector, the sustainability sector or politics/government (to some degree.)

There are also opportunities to champion a cause within less obvious sectors, especially where you may see a particular gap. For example, better work life balance within the legal, education or medical professions. Or making the online world a more conscious and safe space for young adults.

If you take a look at the world of business, you will see how many people have been driven by a cause they were passionate about to take matters into their own hands and set up their own company. The stationery business 'VENT for Change' is one such business which sells sustainable products whilst supporting children's education projects worldwide.

Consider now if there are any causes that particularly drive you.

What needs or problems do you see in the world (or more locally) right now?

What do you see a lack of or where do you see a gap for something?

Which charities have you maybe been keen to support?

Which groups of people do you feel drawn to help champion or support in some way?

Spotting the themes

Having explored the four lines of questioning, I encourage you to now go back through your answers and see if any themes have emerged for you. Are there any common threads running through what you choose to do in your spare time, things you like learning about, what inspires you and the causes you may champion?

Perhaps creativity has come out quite strongly for you? Or maybe the theme of transformation and healing? You may have a number of emerging themes or you may in fact be unable to detect a theme at all. Just surrender to wherever you are at right now. Give yourself some time to reflect on this topic and see what emerges for you in the coming days.

The power of pursuing your passions

Whilst you may not immediately see a way to make a career change which corresponds exactly with one of your passions, I do encourage you to pursue them when you can, because of the wider impact it can have on you and the journey you are on.

Pursuing your passions can support you by:

- Putting you in a more joyful state which will raise your vibration.

- Opening your heart and your mind to something new which could become a potential new career path.

- Signalling your intention to the Universe to bring more passion into your working life.

- Improving your self-worth by honouring your own needs and desires.

- Providing an incentive and an outlet for more balance and wellbeing which can create a more harmonious state from which to realign your career.

I regularly witness a simple act such as a client reading their favourite book just for fifteen minutes a day or giving themselves permission to go to an art gallery or museum once a month make a tangible difference in their lives and to their Career Alignment Journey.

I had one such client who, after going through this exercise, simply felt compelled to pursue her passion for writing (from her Higher Self). She had no clear idea at the time of where it might lead her but she trusted the next steps would unfold. Whilst she didn't yet feel confident or clear of making a big change, she was confident and clear about her writing and following her joy and simply connecting with that. The next step is often the most important one. (She did end up pursuing her calling to transition from a therapist to a creative coach.)

Do stay aware of any limiting beliefs which have or may stop you from pursuing your passions though. Refer back to Chapter 4 to process any negative or unhelpful thought patterns which arise.

Your callings

A calling can mean many things to many people. Traditionally, it has been used to refer to someone entering a religious order in some capacity. I want to offer a broader definition of the word calling here. This definition opens up a whole range of potential career options.

> A calling is a contribution you feel compelled to make in the world.

The word 'calling' implies that there is someone or something doing the calling. This is highly significant if you are on a spiritual path. Pursuing a calling is an opportunity to strengthen your connection with the higher power you believe in by recognising that you have been chosen to carry out a particular mission whilst here on this earth. In a sense, a calling is less about making a choice around what you do and more about *listening for the call* and then choosing whether to respond to that call.

A calling can be identified through a feeling or a physical sensation within the body, for instance:

- A yearning (a deep and intense longing).

- An 'inner pull' towards something.

- Frustration or even pain in relation to a need or a problem in the world.

- Having a clear vision of how things could be different or better.

- A sense of having been 'selected' to carry out a mission.

- A deep inner knowing about a particular path.

One thing which I believe distinguishes a calling is the opportunity to make a *contribution*, to have an impact in the world, whether large or small. Answering a calling can be fulfilling on the deepest level. It is less born out of an ego-based desire, for example, to become famous, and more born out of what the Universe wants to bring into the world *through* you.

However, it is also important to note that answering a calling, or even the mere thought of answering it, can also be accompanied by an intense feeling of resistance or of not being quite ready or good enough. The presence of those thoughts and feelings is not a sign that whatever you are considering is *not* your calling or that you shouldn't pursue it. In fact, quite the opposite. It is often an indication that something *is* your calling and that you have some resistance to work through. The resistance is highlighting that which needs to be healed and answering your calling presents you with the opportunity to do so.

Areas of calling

A calling can come in a variety of shapes and sizes. It doesn't need to be on a grand scale to be meaningful. And it doesn't always require immediately quitting your job or retraining.

You may already have some clarity on a course of action or career path you have felt *called* towards for some time but have never considered in this way until now. Or perhaps, in looking at your passions, you now have some ideas of areas you feel drawn towards investigating as a potential calling.

Whilst a calling is something which comes to you from the Universe, God, Source, the Divine, it can also help to have some ideas presented to you, as a means of acknowledging something existing as a calling or testing your response to a potential calling. You might also see this book and the areas of calling I am about to offer as a way of the Universe communicating to you. As you read through this list, I recommend tuning in to your energy and to any thoughts or feelings which arise.

Also, bear in mind that you may have one very clear calling or you may have one central calling alongside a couple of secondary, inter-connected callings.

A calling could relate to making a contribution in the world through one of these nine areas:

1. *Justice and equality*

Promoting more fairness and morality in the world with issues such as poverty, age, gender or race.

This calling could be responded to in a direct way through the legal profession, by influencing policy or decision makers or working with the social sector on issues such as housing. It may be responded to in a less direct but equally necessary way within organisations such as schools, universities or hospitals, within certain environments, such as corporate head offices or within industries such as the creative industry.

Example career paths: *Charity worker, politics/government, community worker, lobbyist, human rights worker, policy analyst, lawyer/solicitor, social housing officer, diversity and inclusion manager*

2. Beauty and joy

Brightening and uplifting peoples' lives through their senses.

This calling could be fulfilled by offering a product, such as a piece of artwork, a book, a photograph, a greeting card or a handmade piece of furniture, or even through the creation of music or food. You could offer a service which enables people to experience more beauty, such as leading a nature walk or a museum tour. It may even be about helping people enhance or appreciate their own beauty.

Example career paths: *Artist, chef, musician, beautician, photographer, blogger, nature walk leader, interior designer, landscape gardener, architect, designer, florist, food stylist*

3. Wellbeing and healing

Enabling others to improve their health and wellbeing.

This calling includes supporting both physical and mental wellbeing and healing. This could either be in a traditional sense within the healthcare system or it may be about more preventative health care or the growing sector of alternative medicine. It could also involve improving wellbeing within work environments, such as offices or outdoor sites or offering classes to residents within your local area.

Example career paths: *Doctor/nurse, massage therapist, physiotherapist, counsellor, psychotherapist, reiki practitioner, energy healer, yoga teacher, nutritionist, naturopath, sound healer, retreat host, workplace wellbeing manager*

4. Escapism and fun

Lightening peoples' loads by providing a means of escape or entertainment.

This area is about offering people ways to go beyond their normal day-to-day life and into another world or head space. Perhaps you have always felt called to make others laugh or perform in some way. Escapism, such as entertainment, becomes a calling when you understand the deeper impact it can have on others. It could also mean providing a way of escaping within an environment which is more serious or formal but would benefit from introducing an element of fun.

Example career paths: *Actor, comedian, entertainer, dance instructor, podcast host, film-maker, writer, meditation teacher, workshop host*

5. Conservation and preservation

Conserving and protecting nature or buildings for future generations.

This covers a broad area both within the natural world, encompassing the planet's resources, its flora and fauna as well as big issues such as climate change. And also within the man-made world, notably in the heritage sector, for example, historical buildings, museums and archaeology. The common theme is that of ensuring the protection and survival of what we have for future generations.

Example career paths: *Conservationist, ecologist, environmental consultant, forestry commission officer, marine biologist, botanist, recycling/waste management officer, renewable energy consultant, climate change analyst, heritage sector worker, archivist, exhibitions officer, visitor operations officer, fundraiser, archaeologist*

6. Learning and growth

Educating and informing others so they may learn, grow and evolve.

This area of calling covers a multitude of topics, not just within the education sector but also within the world of business, healthcare, personal development and beyond. It may be about helping others learn and grow on an individual basis, a group basis or perhaps to an even wider audience through online courses, webinars, eBooks, podcasts or blogs. You may already know what specific topic you want to focus on, or you may at this stage just have a general sense of being called towards learning and growth.

Example career paths: *Teacher, trainer, lecturer, coach, consultant, podcast host, blogger, author, speaker, forest school practitioner, learning and development manager, facilitator, course creator*

7. Spiritual connection

Guiding others to connect with their spiritual nature and evolve on their spiritual path.

This area of calling might involve helping others with their spiritual wellbeing through a more traditional means which links in with a particular religion. Or perhaps, using a broader definition of spirituality, it's about helping people awaken further on their spiritual path by applying techniques such as the law of attraction or providing a portal into their deeper nature through music or art. It could also be that you provide a product which enables spiritual connection and guidance, for example, crystals or oracle cards.

Example career paths: *Spiritual coach/counsellor, minister, shaman, meditation instructor, spiritual writer, spiritual musician, chaplain, spiritual gift creator/retailer*

8. Protecting and nurturing

Protecting the vulnerable or weak and supporting them in moving forward.

This area of calling can include both animals as well as people. It's about offering shelter and sanctuary either physically or emotionally and believing in others to reach their potential. This might be about protecting and nurturing in a more obvious capacity, such as the paths below or it might be about providing those things within an organisation where you sense it is lacking. Related issues could include homelessness, animal protection, online bullying, teenagers in care or domestic violence.

Example career paths: *Safeguarding officer, youth mentor, social worker, women's refuge centre manager, charity fundraiser or marketeer, animal sanctuary worker*

9. Community and connection

Bringing people together to create connection or a network of support.

This final area of calling is perhaps the most obviously people focused. It's about enabling others to form connections and creating more of a sense of togetherness where it may be lacking. This can be in a direct way such as getting out into the community individually or within a group setting. It could mean playing an active role in an organisation which champions connection, such as a social centre. Or it might be about providing a means of connection through an activity such as a fitness or creative class.

Example career paths: *Community support officer, councillor, social worker, social centre manager, homeless shelter worker, age-related charity worker, class instructor*

My areas of calling

My own calling has mostly been in learning and growth although over recent years it has moved more towards spiritual connection. I have always felt very passionate about the need for more consciousness within the workplace, ever since I experienced the lack of it back in my days in the corporate world. This drives a lot of what I do now, albeit in an indirect way. Through my one-to-one work, I can champion that cause by opening clients up to their own consciousness so that they can bring it to their workplaces.

How to open up to your calling if you still feel unclear

You may have got to this point in the chapter without any clear sense of a possible calling. Or perhaps you may feel confused as to what your main calling is. If so, simply begin *opening up* to your calling, being receptive to it and welcoming it in.

Here are some ways for you to do just that:

- Pay close attention to what you feel drawn to – a book, a podcast, a talk, a course, an event, a person.

- Become more conscious of how an 'inner pull' feels within your own body.

- Engage your Higher Self and your intuition so that you can listen more intently for any signs, nudges or whispers sent to you which might lead you to your calling.

- Ask the Universe for guidance and clarity through prayer and meditation.

Here is a prayer I would like to offer you:

Dear Universe,

I open up to hearing your call.

Let me listen more intently than ever before

Let me notice things which may have escaped my attention

Let me feel it in my bones in a way which leaves me in no doubt

Afford me the faith to believe that I too may have a calling

Afford me the patience to be able to take it one step at a time

Afford me the ability to stay present whilst I'm waiting

Show me how to turn down the volume on other noise

Show me how to follow the trail of my passions

Show me what the world needs from me

I am ready. I am willing.

Aside from living out your calling through a new career path, there may also be opportunities to start opening up to your calling within your current work, or in your life outside of work.

This can be a helpful stepping stone towards a career change into a calling and it enables you to dip your toe in the water if you don't feel totally clear yet. For example, you could:

- Initiate or get involved in a project at work.

- Mentor someone or a group of people in your organisation.

- Champion a change within your workplace or industry.

- Begin a blog to provide inspiration or resources for others.

- Set up a support group online or within your community.

- Connect to your creative side through an activity/hobby.

- Get involved in a local voluntary project.

CHAPTER HIGHLIGHTS

- Your passions and your callings are interconnected – your callings are likely to be derived from those things you are passionate about.

- You can identify your passions by looking at: how you choose to spend your time, what knowledge you love to gain or share, who or what inspires you, what causes you champion.

- Pursuing a passion can have a positive impact on your alignment journey, even if it doesn't turn into a calling.

- A calling is a contribution you feel the Universe is compelling you to make in the world.

- If you don't feel totally clear what your calling is yet, simply open up to the idea and pay attention to where you feel drawn and to your intuition.

- There may be ways to open up to a calling in your current job or life situation which can serve as a stepping stone.

Balance, peace and joy are the fruit of a successful life. It starts with recognising your talents and finding ways to serve others by using them.

THOMAS KINKADE

CHAPTER 11:
Root #4 – Your Gifts

A deep desire to share your gifts with the world and do what brings you joy is inextricably linked with the search for purpose and fulfilment. And so, in this fourth and final root, we will explore what your gifts are by taking an inventory on your transferable skills and your personal qualities. Your skills are essentially the things which you *do* and your qualities are the things which you *are* (your character traits).

Most people only ever look at these when they are applying for a new job or pulling their CV or resume together. Here, we will look at them through a different lens in the context of your Career Alignment Journey. This means that the emphasis will be on the transferable skills and personal qualities which you *enjoy* using or would consciously *choose* to see in your next job description. As a result, there will be a higher vibration behind it.

It can be triggering to think about your own gifts. I often have clients who struggle at the start of this exercise to see themselves as the kind of person who has any gifts or talents. Perhaps because these two words are commonly associated with standing out within such fields as sport, entertainment or art.

In case that is your experience, I want to explain my choice of language here. The word 'gift' simply implies that someone or something has been involved in giving. This opens up the deeper spiritual significance of your skills and your qualities. And it links back to the idea of being a channel for the Universe to work through and the idea that you have been *gifted* certain things in order to carry out your purpose and calling. That could be something outwardly significant such as being a great writer, but it could also be something seemingly less significant, but every bit as impactful, such as the quality of empathy.

A gift can also be a skill or a quality which you have developed or been taught within a particular job. The deeper significance here is that you have been gifted the opportunity to develop this skill or quality. And that this could enable you to pursue your calling.

How recognising your gifts will help you

Taking an inventory on your gifts will provide you with two of the most important ingredients for successfully aligning with your purpose and awakening your career.

Clarity

When you start to truly recognise your gifts – and perhaps the ways in which they have been dampened down in your current situation – it can light a fire inside you which then sparks ideas around how you could use them to make more impact in the world. If you experience any sadness around not having used your gifts yet, I encourage you to firstly honour this feeling and then use it as motivation to make the necessary change.

Taking an inventory on your transferable skills helps you move beyond your current (or most recent) job title by opening your mind up to the breadth of skills you have and therefore the potential for new career paths. After taking this inventory, it may also feel more possible to change careers without the need for extensive retraining.

Through this exercise, you may discover clarity surrounding the question of whether you can find greater happiness and fulfilment within your current job. This has emerged with some of my clients who fully expected to be making a career change through our work together, but once they realised they had all the necessary gifts to be a success where they were, they relaxed into it and found greater fulfilment.

Taking this inventory may also illuminate some areas of development within your current job. Perhaps you have been placed into a role without adequate training and this has been impacting your confidence and happiness. I know lots of people who move through the ranks and get into leadership or managerial roles without ever being taught how to be an effective leader or how to manage a team. So you may be prompted to take an action around asking for more training or mentoring in your current role.

It can be easy to lose sight of your gifts, especially when you have been in a job for a long time. You might even take many of them for granted, perhaps because that is what everyone expects of you or what everyone else is doing in the environment you work in. This is an opportunity to remind yourself and to look at those things objectively, removing yourself from your current environment to see the true value in the gifts you have.

And even if you are not currently working or have been out of paid employment for some time, there will still be many gifts you can draw from within your past work experiences or from life itself.

Confidence

Confidence is another vital ingredient in making a successful career change but accessing it also pays dividends in being able to enjoy the work you might currently be doing. Lack of confidence or imposter syndrome, which manifests as feeling like a 'fraud' at work, is one of the most commonly cited issues with my clients. It can be truly debilitating. I have witnessed some highly talented people tie themselves up in knots because they don't believe they are capable enough to do their job, despite having received glowing feedback or achieving measurable results.

Lack of confidence can have a huge knock-on effect within your working life, such as:

- Experiencing stress and anxiety.

- Not realising your potential.

- Being less effective in your role.

- Taking up head space which could be used to realign with your purpose.

- Creating a low vibration which only attracts more of what you *don't* want into your life.

What would you say your level of confidence is right now? Think about this both in terms of confidence within your current job and also the confidence to make a successful career change.

Owning your gifts

It is one thing to be able to list out your gifts and another thing to be able to truly own them as yours. Demonstrating confidence by taking *ownership* of your gifts can trigger a lot of limiting beliefs and negative thought patterns, often stemming from ego-based fear. Here are some of the common beliefs I come across with my clients:

- If I'm too confident, people won't like me.

- It's arrogant to say that you're good at something.

- It's more important to be humble.

- I'm not as good as other people who do this job.

I encourage you to recognise any fears or limiting beliefs for what they are – simply a product of your Ego Self and nothing more. Your Ego Self is just trying to keep you safe, trying to protect you through these thoughts and beliefs. When you are on a spiritual path, you have the great advantage of being able to call in your Higher Self which offers an alternative view on all of this.

Connecting with your Higher Self allows you to:

- Feel more worthy of any success or praise (whilst acknowledging that you are more than your job anyway).

- Recognise that the gifts you have been given have come from a higher source.

- Understand the deeper significance of your gifts in connection with your purpose and calling.

- Talk about your gifts with a loving, high vibration and without any intention to compete with others or put anyone else down.

- See how your gifts can benefit others and how hiding your light under a bushel benefits no-one.

Inner versus outer confidence

As part of this journey, I want to encourage you to focus on building *inner confidence*. This is something which will provide you with a steady internal anchor. It will help you perform your work – such as meetings, interviews, customer interactions – with greater ease. With inner confidence, you won't need to wait for others to validate what you're good at. You won't be wasting energy and emotion second guessing yourself. And any feedback you do receive can be used simply as a pointer or as something to help you grow.

It is quite common for clients to have a negative association with people who appear to be too confident. This can stop them from being more confident themselves. However, it is often a misperception of confidence based on an *outer* demonstration which is actually deep down coming from a place of fear. For instance, there may be an underlying intent from a colleague to outdo someone else or make them feel small or inadequate by shouting loudly about their own gifts.

What is the difference between inner and outer confidence?

Inner confidence. This is a quiet, assured internal feeling of confidence, which does not depend on any feedback, approval or reassurance from external sources. It's an inner knowing that you can do the job, without any need to remind anyone. You take full ownership of your gifts and feel comfortable talking about them when needed or in the service others.

Outer confidence. This is about how you project yourself externally and how other people perceive you. It's about putting on a confident 'front' when inside you might actually be doubting yourself. Often people can over-compensate a lack of inner confidence by talking in such a way or using body language which masks their inner reality.

Transferable skills

Your transferable skills are those skills which you can take with you from one job and apply in another job. They are therefore of particular significance when considering a career change.

You may also have some industry-specific knowledge or training which you can add to the mix (where relevant) if and when you look to apply for other jobs. Or you may bring these into focus when working on your marketing or sales pitch to attract customers or clients if you decide to become self-employed.

Twelve transferable skills themes

Here is a list of transferable skills grouped into twelve key themes. This is not an exhaustive list, but it does cover many of the key types of transferable skills and provides a start point for your inventory.

As you look at this list, make a note of any of the themes or skills which particularly stand out to you or give you a warm or excited feeling when you consider them. Or equally, those skills which you feel very strongly about *not* wanting to use.

ORGANISATIONAL

planning and organising

project management

goal setting

creating processes

ANALYTICAL

researching

critical thinking

problem solving

generating insights

COMMUNICATION

active listening

writing

speaking

presenting

PEOPLE

influencing

negotiating

emotional intelligence

resolving conflict

TEAM

collaborating

networking

nurturing a team

managing relationships

SUPPORTING

teaching/training

mentoring

coaching

customer service

LEADERSHIP

creating a vision

motivating others

managing change

decision making

COMMERCIAL

selling

marketing

business development

commercial awareness

FINANCIAL

forecasting

budgeting and saving

fund raising

investing

DIGITAL

computer literacy

web development

social media

programming

CREATIVE

designing

innovating

conceptualising

product development

ARTISTIC

making

drawing/painting

performing

photography

What is the overriding feeling or sense you get from initially seeing this list of transferable skills? Does it make you feel different about your current role and your experience? Or about your ability to make a career change?

I had a client who was convinced she had little to offer beyond her role as a lawyer. A mere glance at these skills was enough to jolt her out of her self-deprecating thought pattern and recognise just how much she had to offer the world and also how equipped she already was for self-employment.

A special note on creativity

I want to draw special attention to creativity because of its close link with spirituality. Creativity is the Universe working through you. It is the outer manifestation of your connection to your Higher Self. Often, when you are in the creative flow, it can feel very expansive, very joyful, very meditative. It can take you into another realm where you become the vessel for the Universe to express itself through. This is highly relevant in the context of living your purpose on a spiritual path. In a sense, you are living your purpose just by being creative.

This is why I recommend you tune into your own form of creativity and the ways that you can bring this gift into your life more. Even if, at this stage, it is just through a hobby or some other form of non-paid activity. It will connect you to the Universal Life Force energy stream and bring you some of the fulfilment you are seeking. Plus, it gives you an opportunity to go beyond your thinking mind for a little while!

Personal qualities

Your personal qualities are the attributes or characteristics which form part of who you are. (Note that this is in terms of your *outer* identity, whereas your *inner* identity is your true Divine Nature as we discussed in chapters 5 and 8). Identifying your personal qualities can empower you to make a career change and also build confidence within your current role.

I have chosen to divide the list of personal qualities into what I class as *masculine* qualities and *feminine* qualities. This gives you the opportunity to acknowledge and to honour both aspects of your being – the divine masculine and the divine feminine.

This is not to say that only people identifying as male will demonstrate masculine qualities and only people identifying as female will demonstrate the feminine. But rather, it acknowledges that we all have a combination of both masculine and feminine energy and that when we consciously integrate the two, it accelerates our ability to make a successful transformation.

One example of this is a client who was a highly talented artist and deeply connected to his feminine side (creative, imaginative, free-spirited). But, through conditioning and negative associations with his father, he was unable to integrate his masculine side (being assertive and direct) which was necessary to get his artwork out into the world and enable him to earn a decent living from it. Realising how this was holding him back and releasing the limiting beliefs he held about being more assertive, he was able to let his masculine energy in. Without this, then his beautiful artwork might never have seen the light of day and he may never have fulfilled his purpose and calling to bring more beauty and joy into the world.

In looking at your personal qualities in this way, it also gives you the opportunity to acknowledge the feminine qualities you have which may have been overlooked in certain work environments in favour of the masculine. Qualities such as compassion, sensitivity and empathy are rarely encouraged or celebrated in the same way as being analytical, logical and resolute. And yet these are the sorts of qualities which are now needed in the world more than ever before.

As you look at the two lists of qualities I will now share with you, I invite you to see which ones resonate with you, which ones trigger you and which ones you maybe wish you had more of.

MASCULINE		FEMININE	
action-oriented	independent	adaptable	imaginative
adventurous	logical	articulate	intuitive
ambitious	objective	authentic	kind
analytical	persistent	caring	loving
assertive	practical	collaborative	loyal
authoritative	professional	compassionate	nurturing
confident	progressive	conscientious	open-minded
courageous	protective	cooperative	passionate
decisive	realistic	creative	patient
direct	resilient	dependable	playful
discerning	resolute	empathetic	receptive
disciplined	resourceful	encouraging	sensitive
driven	responsible	expressive	sensuous
dynamic	risk-taker	flexible	sincere
efficient	self-assured	free-spirited	supportive
energetic	self-motivated	friendly	thoughtful
fearless	stable	generous	trustworthy
firm	stoic	gentle	understanding
focused	straight-forward	helpful	vulnerable
grounded	tenacious	humble	warm

Taking your inventory

Having looked at some transferable skills and personal qualities, we can now dive into the inventory itself. As with your values, rather than ask you to list out all your transferable skills and personal qualities, we are going to see them in context and illicit them more naturally by looking at your:

- Experience
- Feedback
- Challenges
- Successes

I recommend working through this chronologically so that you can structure your thoughts and don't miss anything. We will then narrow that down into your top five transferable skills and your top five personal qualities.

Download your free Gifts Worksheet in the Book Resources, which you can access through this link:

rebeccakirk.co.uk/book-resources

1. Experience

In your journal, list out your previous jobs, the roles you've played or the projects you've been involved in, including those linked to any non-work activities. Then make a note of the transferable skills you've gained and the personal qualities you've demonstrated in each of those. It might help to consider what transferable skills and personal qualities would be listed in the job description if that role was being advertised.

Here are a few examples of some roles outside of paid work and the associated transferable skills and personal qualities:

- Being captain of a sports team could demonstrate your leadership and teamwork skills alongside your collaborative or nurturing qualities.

- Coordinating a voluntary project could demonstrate your project management and motivational skills alongside your caring and compassionate qualities.

- Setting up a blog to share your travel experiences could demonstrate your writing and computer skills alongside your expressive and adventurous qualities.

Are there any common themes within your list of transferable skills and personal qualities? Which transferable skills and personal qualities are your favourites on this list?

2. Feedback

If you are spending a lot of your head space focusing on your *current* work situation and feel like you lack the necessary abilities to make a career change, you may have lost sight of the impact you have had on others over the years. Often, the brain naturally looks at the things which didn't go so well or our perceived failings. It can be easy to forget some of the positive feedback you may have received over the course of your life and career.

Reflect on any positive feedback you have had from others including colleagues, customers, clients, teachers and managers. This could be in the form of verbal or written feedback, however seemingly insignificant.

Consider the following and extract any transferable skills and personal qualities which the feedback highlights:

- Emails from colleagues

- Thank you notes from customers

- Past performance reviews

- Testimonials or client reviews

- Ad hoc conversations with colleagues (for example, following a presentation or a meeting)

Dig deep and see how much you can recall or unearth out of your office drawers or your inbox. And if you haven't had any feedback to draw on, it doesn't mean that you don't have any skills or qualities!

I want to end this section with another caveat. Feedback is useful here in the context of drawing out insights from comments which you have *already* received. However, in line with what I discussed on inner confidence, I encourage you not to hook yourself in to receiving feedback going forward.

3. Challenges

It is not just experiences within work which can be drawn from for this inventory. Often, our life experiences and challenges can be our greatest teachers and therefore also a rich source of transferable skills and personal qualities.

Consider what challenges you have had in your life and which transferable skills or personal qualities each one demonstrates. This could include, for instance:

- Moving to live in another country which demonstrates organisational skills and risk-taking plus the qualities of adaptability and courage.

- Managing a health challenge which highlights an ability to handle problems as well as demonstrating resilience.

- Coming through a relationship break-up which highlights skills at resolving conflict and building new connections as well as a positive and adaptable nature.

4. Successes

Your successes can also hold the key to knowing what some of your gifts are. When I use the word 'success', I am referring to your *own* definition of success here rather than a societal definition, such as reaching the top of the career ladder, having 2.4 children, living in a big house with an expensive car or having thousands of followers.

Here are the types of successes you could draw from:

- Leaving a job which you had felt trapped in and overcoming the fear of change – demonstrating decision making, determination and courage.

- Enabling a team member to gain a promotion – demonstrating nurturing and mentoring skills.

- Attaining a qualification whilst also working full-time – demonstrating discipline, initiative and effective time management.

- Making a piece of artwork for a family member's birthday – demonstrating creativity and thoughtfulness.

- Helping a friend to come through a difficult time and restart their life – demonstrating empathy, compassion and supportiveness.

- Reaching a charity fundraising target – demonstrating organisational skills alongside tenacity and generosity.

- Getting fit enough to run a half marathon – demonstrating self-motivation and focus.

What do you consider to be your successes, either in or out of work? What things are you most proud of? What achievements demonstrate your application of a particular skill or quality? Again, these could be perceived as big or small.

Consider the people who you might serve in your organisation and the contribution you make to your colleagues, clients, customers, students or patients. Also consider the contribution you make to the people in your network of friends and family.

Your top five gifts

Now that you have taken your inventory, it's time to create some focus and draw out some insights from what you have uncovered. To create a shift and undo the patterns of previous jobs, it is important to tune into the gifts which you actually *enjoy* using, the ones which light you up. They are the ones which make you feel most alive, most in alignment and most able to make an impact in the world – and the ones which you might actually want to see listed on your ideal job description, even if you aren't totally clear yet what that job is.

Take a look now back through all of the transferable skills and personal qualities you have listed and consider which transferable skills and personal qualities fall into that category. Highlight your top five transferable skills and your top five personal qualities.

As you do this, connect with your intuition and sense how each of these feels in your body as you scan your list. Anything which gives you a warm sensation or an inner knowing or 'rightness' is confirmation that this is indeed one of your top gifts.

Your superpower

I now challenge you to narrow down your list further into your one biggest gift – your 'superpower'. What is that one special skill or quality that you sense has been bestowed upon you from the Universe to use in this lifetime? What is that gift unique to you which you could use to make the most difference in the world? What have you perhaps been given to help carry out your calling?

CHAPTER HIGHLIGHTS

- Sharing your gifts is inextricably linked to understanding and living your purpose.

- From a spiritual perspective, you have been *gifted* certain transferable skills and personal qualities in order to carry out your purpose and calling.

- Highlighting your gifts brings clarity and confidence either for a career change or improving your current job.

- It is important to tune into the gifts which you actually *enjoy* using.

- Developing *inner* confidence will provide you with an internal anchor and help you navigate a career change.

- Integrating your masculine and feminine qualities creates a potent mix to make a transformation.

Journalling questions

How possible do you believe it is to share your gifts and live out more of your purpose within your current work situation?

What ideas has this exercise sparked around an alternative career path (or paths) which align with your top five gifts? Write anything down which comes to mind, without judgement.

What has this exercise highlighted to you in terms of your own perceptions of your abilities?

Taking into consideration all the transferable skills and personal qualities you have listed, how would you score your level of confidence in your ability to do your current job, on a scale of one to ten where ten is the most confident?

How would you score your confidence in your ability to make a successful career change, on a scale of one to ten where ten is the most confident?

Looking at your gifts, how much are you able to truly 'own' them as yours? What thoughts or feelings does this perhaps trigger in you?

If you have an alternative career path already in mind, how much will your identified transferable skills and personal qualities help you in pursuing that?

What new skills or qualities might you choose to gain to support you in living your purpose more in your current role?

What new skills or qualities might you choose to gain to support you in living your purpose more through a new career path?

PART 4:
ALIGNING YOUR CAREER

The only thing scarier than going down a new career path is staying stuck on your current one and living to regret it.

REBECCA KIRK

CHAPTER 12:
Moving Through your Career Crossroads

We are now at the 'business end' of your Career Alignment Journey. It's time to start drawing together all the learnings and insights you have generated over the previous chapters, clarifying your options and working up a plan for you to move forward with.

The energy behind Part 4 of this book may feel very different to earlier sections. This is now the action phase of your journey where things start to feel a bit more 'real'. You might be ready for this now, or you might choose to come back to this section, after a period of further reflection. Listen within as to what feels right for you.

I do have a word of caution for you though. Do not put off working through this final section through fear or to avoid any discomfort which may come from making decisions and moving into action. Grab your journal and let out any thoughts, fears or beliefs that you may have about narrowing your options down and contemplating leaving the relative safety of your current nest.

I also encourage you to stay connected to your intuition to guide you through this section. Be aware of how the different options which emerge for you *feel* in your body and in your heart. That is your inbuilt guidance system and now is the time it can really come into its own and support you.

The Career Alignment Pathways

We begin by taking a step back from the detail and taking things up a level. We are going to put you right in the heart of your career crossroads with a view to making a choice on which 'Career Alignment Pathway' you are going to begin journeying on.

I want you to imagine right now that you have gone for a walk in a forest. The pathway you have been treading for a while is starting to feel a little uncomfortable and you don't have any motivation to go much further. You reach an opening in the forest where there are three different pathways you can choose.

- You can **stay** on the pathway you are already on which is reassuringly familiar and safe, have a little recharge and change into more comfortable shoes so that the rest of your journey feels lighter.

- You can take a totally **new** and unchartered pathway, adventuring into an undiscovered part of the forest, with the potential to see new wildlife or a beautiful view, but also with a risk of getting lost or coming across some scary creatures.

- You can veer off your current pathway via a **stepping stone** which moves you towards the adventurous new path to catch a glimpse of some new sights, whilst also staying close by to more familiar and safe surroundings.

Which pathway are you instinctively drawn to taking on your walk through the forest? This an analogy for your career crossroads.

We will now take a look at each of those pathways in relation to your career. The chart on the next page illustrates what each pathway involves and the ways in which they interconnect

By the end of the next few chapters, my hope that you are at least clear on which of those three pathways you feel most drawn to taking at this point in time.

Even if there seems only one obvious pathway to you right now, I still encourage you to read about the other two, so that you can very consciously and symbolically let go of them, enabling you to create some necessary head space.

THE THREE CAREER ALIGNMENT PATHWAYS

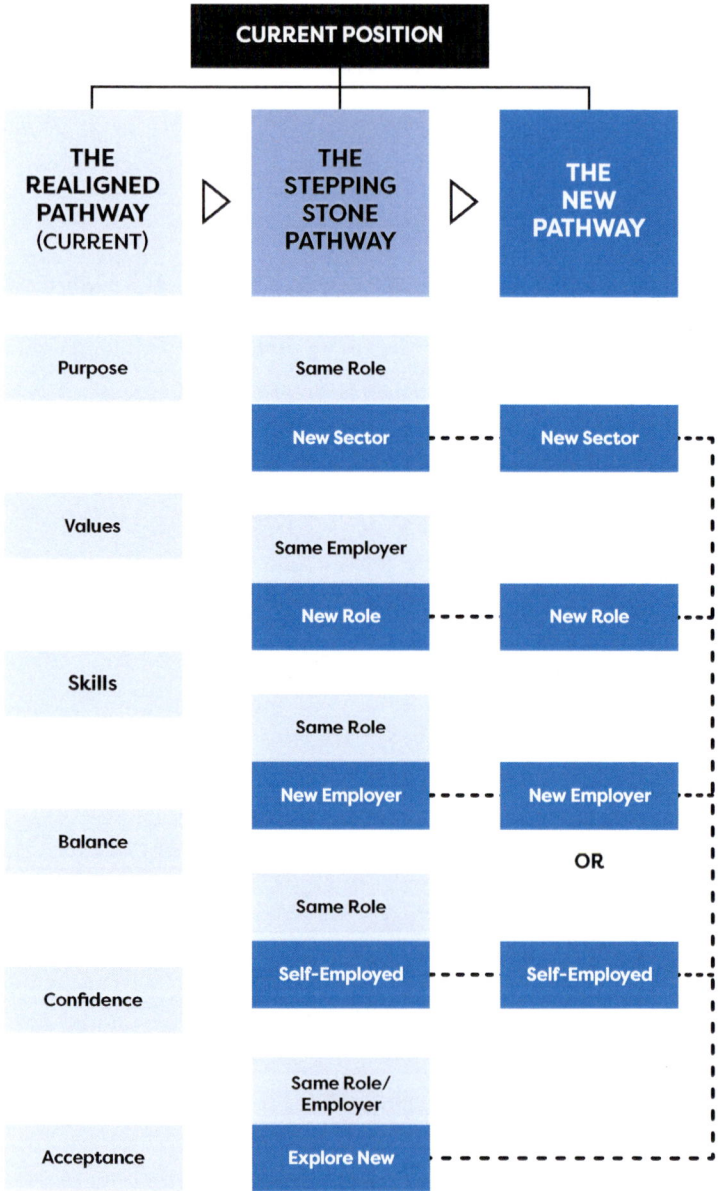

The Realigned Pathway (current)

As I have said from the very start of the book, it may be possible for you to find what you are looking for by staying in your current role and making some changes which bring you into closer alignment with your True Self. This process may have helped you to realise that there is some *inner* work to be done rather than seeking career fulfilment and happiness just by making *outer* changes. (If you are not currently in a role, you can instead view this pathway as staying in your current *situation*.)

Taking the path of realigning with your current career can also be used as a temporary measure or as a strategy for making your working life more bearable whilst you:

- Gain more clarity on the way forward with one of the other pathways.

- Address a need to prioritise one of your top ten values for a period of time, for example, financial security.

- Wait for your longer-term plan (to move into something new) to come into fruition.

You may have already gone past the point of this pathway being a viable option. Perhaps your intuition is screaming out to you that you need to make a more significant change. Or maybe you just feel it in every fibre of your being that you have already exhausted every possible way of improving things in your current role.

If you know deep down that this pathway isn't going to work for you, I invite you to formally acknowledge this now. By letting this pathway go, you will then be able to create time and space (both mentally and energetically) to focus more fully on the pathway you *do* want to take and to manifest the change you yearn for.

If you do choose this pathway, I encourage you to spend some time exploring very honestly your reasons for taking it and whether it is out of fear of making a bigger change. Only take this path because it feels like there is genuine potential for you to feel more aligned and to live out more of your potential after making some changes. You might find it helpful to call on your Higher Self to support you.

Drawing on the learnings and insights from previous chapters, these are some of the ways in which you might be able to realign with your current career.

Purpose

In Chapter 7, we explored the idea of bringing more of a sense of purpose to your current job by reminding yourself of the people or the cause you ultimately serve and reconnecting with your employer. And also, the idea that you might choose to show up to your work in a new way, such as spreading more love and more light to the people you interact with. As part of this pathway, perhaps you can reconsider *how* you do your job versus *what* job you do, so you are able to make more impact.

In Chapter 10 we explored the concept of being 'called' to serve within a particular area. Are you already working in a role that encompasses your calling? If this is true, then simply recognising that you can fulfil your purpose in your current role could help you to realign.

You might also consider new ways to bring more purpose into your working life as a whole, through activities such as volunteering or passions such as creativity, or through connecting with your Life Purpose or Higher Purpose.

In what ways might you be able to align with more purpose within your current working life?

Values

In Chapter 9 we looked at your most important values and the things in life which deeply motivate you. Once they have been brought to light and steps have been taken or put in place towards honouring your values, it can be possible to find more peace and happiness within your existing job.

Let's say, for example, autonomy is in your top ten list of values and you only scored it a three in terms of how much of it you have right now. If your boss or employer is willing to make some changes which give you greater license to make your own decisions or work in a way which gives you more breathing space, it might mean that you can enjoy your current job a whole lot more.

Similarly, if the value of creativity is important to you and currently missing from your working life, you might find that honouring this by making time for creative pursuits in your weekly schedule brings a spark back which also has a positive knock-on effect on your work.

How much better would you feel about staying in your current job if you were able to align more with your values?

Gifts

It might simply be the case that you are not using your gifts in your current job. This may be creating an underlying feeling of frustration or despondency as you sense your true potential going to waste. It might feel like there is so much more you could be doing or you may feel like you have not been properly trained to do the job you are doing, and that your effectiveness and happiness are being impacted as a result.

Before you make a change outside of your current job, consider for a moment the possibility of changing things within it. For example, imagine being able to:

- Use more of your favourite skills and personal qualities.

- Learn a new skill which enables you to be more confident and effective in your role, for example, giving presentations.

- Develop a new strength which you have always yearned for, for example, assertiveness.

What this requires is firstly an openness on your part to the *possibility* of change within your current role. And secondly, a conversation with your employer to explore the options for you to use more of your gifts or to embark on some skills training or mentoring.

Consider now which of your top five transferable skills and personal qualities you may be able to bring more of into your current role. Is there an opportunity to work on a project which would tap into your creative side? Could you begin mentoring a junior colleague and share your gift of empathy? Is there a training course on leadership which would allow you to be a more effective manager?

How likely would you be to stick with your current role if you used more of your gifts, felt more equipped to do a good job or were able to learn and grow more?

Balance

How might you feel about your current job if you were able to create and maintain a more balanced working life? Feelings of stress and overwhelm can often cloud our judgement and lead us towards making choices from a heightened emotional state which may not be for our highest good. And, if left unchecked, poor work life balance and the inability to manage your stress or properly prioritise could also follow you to your next job.

Consider how much more sustainable and enjoyable your current working life might be if you knew how to:

- Set and maintain boundaries so you could properly switch off from work.

- Put your own wellbeing into the mix both at work and at home.

- Have a daily practice which instilled a sense of calm and inner peace.

- Allow yourself time and space outside of work for things which light you up.

It might be that you choose to give this a go as a short-term goal which we look at in the final chapter.

How might you feel about staying in your current job if you were to have a more balanced and less stressful working life?

Confidence

How much happier and calmer might you feel in your current role if you:

- Fully owned your gifts?

- Stopped suffering from imposter syndrome?

- Had an inner confidence which meant you weren't dependent on what others thought?

- Called on your Higher Self more and learnt to quieten your Ego Self?

Sometimes when a client comes to me longing for a career change, what is at the root of that longing is actually a lack of confidence. The career change is often an unconscious escape plan from dealing with this deeper issue. Again, this is something which could just follow you around and into your next job if you don't confront it in your current one.

It might be possible, using the tools we have explored, to gain more confidence in your current job and thereby negate the need to make a bigger, outer change. Consider now what actions you could take to boost your confidence in the role that you do, such as practices to connect you to your Higher Self, repeating a daily mantra which reframes any limiting beliefs about yourself, or a reminder of your top transferable skills and personal qualities.

How much more aligned or at peace might you be in your current job if you felt more confident within yourself and released any doubts about your abilities?

Acceptance

Acceptance is a subtle but powerful practice which can shift your energy in an instant and help you to realign with your current job. In the context of your career, it's about acknowledging the aspects of your job which are less than ideal, and cannot be changed, and accepting them for what they are. This doesn't mean that you must *like* them but what it does mean is that you don't waste any further energy or head space fighting against them or trying to change them. This can create feelings of greater peace and harmony.

The opportunities to practice acceptance within your current job could be in relation to:

- The people you work with whom you perhaps find challenging, such as your boss.

- Certain tasks which you don't enjoy doing, provided this doesn't make up a large percentage of your time.

- The need you have to prioritise a certain value right now, such as financial security, which means you stay where you are rather than making a career change.

You can practice acceptance through use of a daily affirmation or by cultivating an in-the-moment awareness of when you feel triggered and then calling in the subtle, peaceful energy of acceptance.

How would it impact your daily working life and your ability to stay in your current role if you were able to practice greater acceptance?

I worked with a client who was a head of department in a private school. In our last session when we reflected on the journey he had been on, he commented, "If you had told me at the start of this process that I would end up finding more happiness in the same job, I would not have believed you". What was unearthed through our sessions was how much he was lacking in confidence to do his job and an underlying belief that he was not worthy of it. His connection to purpose was there. This career already had meaning to him. But his uncomfortable emotions had clouded over this and led him to believe that he needed to change his career. He still had a longer-term aim to move into a different type of role within the education sector, but in the short- and medium-term, he was resolved in feeling more fulfilled and making the most of the opportunity to realise more of the potential right in front of him.

The New Pathway

The New Pathway is one where you make a complete change to all aspects of your career – the sector, the role and the employer. You embark on a journey of self-discovery into unchartered territory.

We will explore each of the aspects of your potential new career in the next chapter so that you can gain some clarity on what this pathway might look like for you.

This pathway might be the best option for you if you:

- Are ready for a fresh start and a new challenge.

- Know what your Career Purpose is.

- Have the time and the finances to get started on your new path.

- Have taken or explored the other pathways and are still feeling unfulfilled.

- Feel deeply called towards this pathway by your Higher Self.

If you answered yes to any of those, if you have done your due diligence by working through the exercises in this book, and if you are ready to create a significant step-change in your career and in your life, then this is the pathway I would recommend.

The benefits of taking this pathway include:

- Having more time and focus to make your new career a success.

- Welcoming in a fresh new energy which comes from making a clean break.

- Having built-in motivation to make it happen as you don't have your old work or income stream to fall back on.

- Negating the risk of talking yourself out of it which can happen during an extended period of planning or transitioning.

This pathway can be a scary proposition. Entering a brand-new sector and doing something you've never done before, possibly involving retraining or setting up your own business may feel exciting but also terrifying and overwhelming. This feeling is normal. And it doesn't need to stop you.

I do want to acknowledge that not everyone will feel like they have the means of taking this pathway right now. This may be due to financial reasons, especially if there is significant investment involved in retraining. It could also be due to life circumstances, especially those which significantly impact your time and head space such as a house move or a new baby.

This is where transitioning into a new career over time could offer you a more manageable route forward. The New Pathway might be something which you work towards by, for example, setting some savings goals or continuing to earn from your current job during a period of retraining. This will be considered when we look at your Career Alignment Plan in Chapter 14.

But for those of you who feel the time is right and who have a deep inner yearning to make a complete career change, I encourage you to embrace the fear and do it anyway. Fear will be a part of this journey you are on. Accept that. See it as an opportunity for deep personal growth. Yes, there is risk in making a career change, but what is the risk involved in *not* making one? How would that impact you (physically, emotionally, spiritually)? And if not now, then when?

Fiona's story

Fiona came to me after working for 23 years as an accountant and feeling deeply unhappy. "I no longer felt fulfilled in the job that I was doing. I'd built my career, progressing from a finance clerk to a finance director. Reaching the top of my game, I didn't have the feeling that I thought I should have."

Following a career break and investing time working through the tools and concepts in this book together, Fiona decided to take the plunge and follow a life-long ambition and a deep calling to become a dance instructor. Having never worked for herself before and with no prior experience in this sector, Fiona took the leap and here is what she has since found.

"Financially I've had to make sacrifices and I am challenged almost every day as I navigate self-employment and explore my own creativity in my career but I have a sense of freedom that I've never felt before. I am empowered to make my own decisions and take opportunities. I have a new level of confidence and self-esteem that cannot be shattered by anyone. I lost the fear and found my purpose and I am being my authentic self every day. That is such a wonderful feeling. I love what I do and even though I might not know exactly where I'm heading, I'm not scared, I'm excited, I'm not lost, I have a purpose and with a new spiritual connection to myself and the Higher Self, I trust in the process. I am living my authentic self and that feels so wonderfully freeing. I couldn't look back."

How drawn do you feel to choosing this pathway and making a complete career change?

What would the benefits be for you in choosing this option?

What do you see as the drawbacks of you choosing this pathway?

The Stepping Stone Pathway

This third pathway offers you a halfway house between the other two – between the known and the unknown. It provides you with a manageable way of realigning with your purpose by transitioning *away* from your current situation and moving *towards* a brand-new career.

You may choose this pathway if you are feeling acutely overwhelmed by making a full career change at this time. It might be that you have unchangeable time or financial constraints you need to take into account, or that you need more time to explore a totally different path.

The benefits this pathway offers are that:

- It provides you with a less risky way forward than a complete career change.

- It will allow for a quicker change, if you don't need to retrain.

- You can take advantage of your existing experience and contacts.

- It enables you to prepare for a complete career change, for example, by starting to save money.

Whilst the Stepping Stone Pathway is a more strategic option, it is also possible that it could become fulfilling in and of itself. If you consciously draw on your four roots, there is the potential to align your career with the purpose and fulfilment you are seeking.

How this pathway works

With the Stepping Stone Pathway, basically you begin aligning with your purpose by changing *one* aspect of your current career whilst maintaining another. For example, changing the sector you work in but doing the same role. Or changing your role within the same employer. It might also mean continuing with your current job *alongside* exploring a potential new career path – say through volunteering, focusing more on your hobby business or making time for one of your passions.

Change your sector

It may be possible for you to find more fulfilment by doing the same role but within a new sector. This can be a good stepping stone option where your current line of work is easily transferable. Say, for instance, you're a digital marketeer and you're keen to move into the wellbeing sector. You could look for a marketing role within the wellbeing sector which allows you to get a foot in the door and understand more about the sector before making a bigger leap into your ultimate role.

This kind of step can also help you to gain further clarity on what the right role might be. Or you may find that using your skills and experience in a more aligned way like this and enabling others to improve their wellbeing is enough to bring you the fulfilment you are seeking.

What opportunities are there for you to find greater fulfilment by doing a similar role within a new sector which aligns more with your roots?

Change your role

It may be that you have an opportunity within your current organisation to move into a more aligned role. Ultimately you may wish to be doing this role for a different employer, within a different sector or perhaps working for yourself. But it is often an easier transition to make with an existing employer as you are already a known entity. This option is typically more viable within a larger organisation where there is more scope to move departments or even to carve out a brand new role.

I had a client who wanted to work for herself as an events organiser within the arts sector. She was working at the time for a global FMCG (fast-moving consumer goods) manufacturer as a brand manager. She had the scope to move into a role there as a corporate events manager which gave her the opportunity to gain experience as well as an important insight into this new role from the safety of an organisation she already knew and trusted.

What opportunities are there with your current employer to move into a more aligned role?

Change your employer

Perhaps you could do the same role within the same sector but move to a new employer. You might consider this, firstly, as part of a longer-term career change strategy where the new employer has broader reach into other sectors and/or into other roles. The new employer could open doors for you which otherwise may be more difficult to unlock.

Secondly, it could be that you move to a new employer who is just more aligned with your own values and purpose. One with a different culture or style of leadership which allows you to thrive more.

For example, say you are an accountant working for one of the Big Four firms but you feel out of alignment with their corporate values. Moving to an independent family-run accounting firm where you feel like you can make more of a difference and have closer connections with your clients might be just the ticket to bring more fulfilment into your working life.

Which other employers in your industry might be a better fit with your values?

Which employers might provide a stepping stone for you to test out other more aligned roles or sectors further down the line?

Become self-employed

Although not possible with all jobs, there may be the option of doing what you do now but by working for yourself. This could enable you to learn the ropes of running your own business whilst doing a job and working within a sector which are both already familiar to you. It can also offer a very direct route to aligning with certain values such as freedom, autonomy and flexibility.

Certain lines of work lend themselves well to self-employment.

For example, professional roles which can be performed in a consulting or freelance capacity, such as marketing, design, or brand development. And similarly, skilled work, such as the work of a beautician, a software developer or a writer/journalist.

It may be that you can discover the fulfilment you are seeking just from making this change. Or it could be that such a change provides you with a platform to learn the necessary skills of entrepreneurship such as marketing, financial management and networking, which can later be applied in a totally new role.

What are the possibilities for self-employment within your current or previous line of work?

How might this provide you with a stepping stone to move your career forward?

Explore a new career path alongside your current

You might instead choose to actively test out a potential new career path whilst remaining in your current job. This enables you to maintain an income and work towards getting further clarity on what the New Career Pathway might look like for you. You can explore a potential new career path through volunteering, through setting up a side business or through spending time pursuing one of your passions. Or it may be that you take a qualification or embark on a period of study in a new field in order to test the waters or enable you to make a career change further down the line.

An important factor in making this option work is the ability to carve out time in your schedule. Some of my clients have managed to do this by reducing their hours to part time and setting aside one day per week to focus on studying.

How might you be able to actively explore a new career path whilst staying in your current job?

What might need to change for this to be a viable option for you?

My pathway to becoming a coach

This Stepping Stone Pathway is the route which I first took when I left my corporate retail job and before I made the ultimate leap into coaching. When I took my career break in Sydney back in 2010, I never planned to come out of it having set up my own business. But, after doing some deep reflective work over there, it felt like the most natural and obvious next step for me to take. I felt very drawn and motivated to sharing my skills and experience with small businesses and brands who needed support. And I was keen to dip my toe in the water with self-employment. So I set myself up as a retail and brand consultant working with creative entrepreneurs as well as some well-known high street retailers.

At the time, I didn't realise I wanted to become a coach (even though I can see now that the signs were already there). Moving into self-employment represented a significant change to me and most definitely allowed me to align more with my values of freedom, balance, personal growth and making a difference.

Everything which I learnt about running my own business during that time became truly invaluable to me when I made my career change into coaching. It meant that I was already au fait with the ins and outs of such things as managing my financial accounts and setting up and maintaining a website. When I retrained as a coach, I could, in a sense, hit the ground running.

Just take the next step

The main point I want to land with this pathway is that you can take your career change in stages. You don't have to figure it all out at once or (if you have figured it out) make the leap all at once. Just change something.

And if you feel drawn to this pathway, again I encourage you to sense check what might be behind it. To ask yourself the question as to whether you are choosing this pathway out of fear of taking the New Pathway. Or whether, in connection with your Higher Self, it intuitively feels like the right option for you right now.

How might you benefit from choosing a Stepping Stone Pathway?

What are the potential drawbacks for you in choosing this pathway?

Choosing a pathway

Now we have taken a look at all three Career Alignment Pathways, I invite you to take another look at the summary chart and reflect on which feels like the best option for you right now. And whether you need more information to make a considered choice.

It can be very freeing to consciously let go of one or more of the pathways. Say, for instance, you have spent a lot of time thinking about whether to leave your current job, if this now feels like it is not a viable option, then release it now. Make space for the new to enter.

CHAPTER HIGHLIGHTS

- It may be possible to find more happiness and fulfilment by realigning with your current role.

- The New Pathway provides a powerful fresh start and a huge opportunity for personal growth but also requires embracing any fear.

- The Stepping Stone Pathway offers a manageable way to transition from your current to a future new career path, and can be fulfilling in and of itself.

- Even if you feel strongly about one pathway, there is still value in acknowledging and releasing the other two.

- Be honest with yourself about your choice of pathway and sense check that it is not coming from a place of fear.

Your work is to clarify and purify your vision so that the vibration that you are offering can then be answered.

ESTHER HICKS

CHAPTER 13:
Clarifying your Aligned Career Path

Much of your Career Alignment Journey so far has been building up to this chapter – pinpointing exactly what your aligned career path looks like. We will now begin harnessing any existing ideas, and generating some potential new ones by pinpointing the finer detail of your pathway.

Focusing in this way will be especially helpful if you have decided to take either the New or Stepping Stone Pathways. But it can also be of value if you have decided to stay in your current position with the Realigned Pathway, by allowing you to sense check your alignment with your four roots. And if you aren't yet sure which pathway to take, this chapter will help you further in deciding which way to go.

The Purpose Tree revisited

In the Purpose Tree I shared with you in Chapter 7, we explored how your aligned career path, the trunk of the tree, emerges naturally from the firm planting of your four roots. We will now revisit the Purpose Tree with a view to drawing together all of your insights and learnings.

Capturing everything in one place in this way means that you can more easily spot any themes or connections which may lead you to a specific career choice. It may also be that this exercise substantiates any ideas you have already had and reassures you that they are indeed in alignment with your roots. Plus, it will serve as a reminder of all the great work you have done!

For your Higher Self root, I suggest you note the character traits which you identified with in Chapter 8 which will support you in aligning your career. For example, authentic, abundant, expansive. Or you might want to make a simple statement which connects you with your Higher Self and with your potential. For example, "I am creative, I am powerful, I am worthy."

Also, state your prosperity goal at the top of the tree, as this can act as a powerful source of motivation and a reminder of the prize on offer from aligning your career. This goal might be a certain amount of income you would like to earn, or it could be something less tangible such as fulfilment or inner peace.

Have a go now and fill out your Purpose Tree and see what emerges for you.

Download your free Purpose Tree Worksheet in the Book Resources, which you can access through this link:

rebeccakirk.co.uk/book-resources

What connections can you make between the different roots of?

What ideas have emerged for you around potential career paths which align with your roots?

Pratesh's story

One of my clients had toyed with the idea throughout our sessions of setting up his own decluttering business and helping people in later life to let go of their possessions in preparation for passing on. This is what he noted in his Purpose Tree.

- My values: community, connection, orderliness, creativity, inner peace.

- My gifts: organising, communicating, empathising, attention to detail, helping others.

- My passions and callings: community and connection, working with the elderly.

- My Higher Self: I am focused on growth, I am authentic, I am calm.

When Pratesh looked at his tree and drew the connections between the different roots, it was obvious to him that this business idea was in full alignment. It gave him the opportunity to serve and connect with her community and honour his love of orderliness. Working with the elderly and their families at this stage of their life also meant he could use his gift of empathy whilst enabling them to experience greater inner peace.

Narrowing down your aligned career path

Another approach to help you generate ideas for your next role (or to go deeper with any ideas you already have) is to break down the different aspects of a potential new career path into:

- The sector

- The role

- The employer (or self-employment)

Again, alignment is key here so it is important that these aspects are sense-checked against the four roots of your Purpose Tree.

The sector

The sector is the grouping of job types or industry category. As a start point, it is useful to be clear on which sectors you are most drawn to.

Here is a list of different career sectors to consider:

CAREER SECTORS

Administration

Animal care

Architecture

Arts

Beauty

Business operations and management

Charity and not-for-profit

Children's services

Construction

Creative industries

Distribution and logistics

Entertainment

Engineering

Energy

Environment and conservation

Education and training

Emergency services

Farming, forestry and fishing

Fashion

Finance

Government and public sector

Healthcare

Heritage

Hospitality and tourism

IT and digital

Law

Manufacturing

Marine and maritime

Marketing and advertising

Media, publishing and journalism

Military

Personal development

Property and housing

Retail

Science and technology

Security

Social care and community services

Sports

Wellbeing, including spirituality

Telecommunications

Transport

The sector(s) you choose will be largely driven out by your preferred area of calling, which you identified in Chapter 10.

Here are some examples of how a career sector can directly relate to an area of calling:

- Career sectors which would allow you to follow a calling into the area of **protecting and nurturing** might include social care or children's services.

- Career sectors which would allow you to follow a calling into the area of **learning and growth** might include education and training or personal development.

- Career sectors which would allow you to follow a calling into the area of **beauty and joy** might include the arts, beauty or entertainment.

As I touched on in Chapter 10, there may be a less obvious link between an area of calling and a sector. For instance, you may be called to bring greater justice and equality into the finance sector or to bring more wellbeing and healing into the retail sector – that is, to places where you might deem these things to be currently lacking.

Which sector(s) do you feel most drawn to from the list?

Which sector(s) connect you most with your calling?

How do you feel about the sector you are currently in (or have most recently been in)?

The role

Now let's get a little more clarity on the type of role which might be the best fit for you within the sector(s) you have identified. There are two ways you can go about this. You can explore what roles are actually available within your preferred sectors before then sense checking how much they align with your roots. Whilst it is beyond the scope of this book to list here all the thousands of jobs which are available within each sector, here are some suggestions to get you started with your own research.

- Do an online search for roles within the sector you are considering. For example, 'roles within the heritage sector'.

- Take a look at the National Careers Service website in the UK or your country's equivalent which lists out a number of jobs within a range of sectors.

- Speak to anyone you may know who works within a certain sector to gain an understanding around the types of roles which exist.

- Research any relevant associations or governing bodies within the sector. For example, The British Association for Counselling and Therapy if you're considering a counselling career. Visit their website or obtain an industry publication to browse their jobs pages.

- Visit the careers page of the website of a sector leader or well-known organisation. For example, the BBC within broadcasting, the NHS within healthcare, the RSPCA within the charity sector.

- Do a filtered search on a job platform such as Monster or the website of a recruitment agency which is specific to the sector you are looking at.

- Search the online careers pages of any preferred employers you might identify in the section below.

Alternatively, or additionally, you can 'create' your ideal aligned role, on paper, by answering five key questions which enable you to clarify your vision. Your vision can be used in the manifestation exercise recommended as part of your Career Alignment Plan in the final chapter.

Make sure that you don't slip into any negative thinking or recite any limiting beliefs around what is possible. Let your mind and your heart be free to dream.

1. What gifts do you want to be able to use?

Imagine you were looking at your ideal job description. What might be some of the transferable skills and personal qualities you would love to see on there? Which of your gifts are you looking to use more of as part of your purpose?

For example:

- Motivating others
- Mentoring and supporting
- Designing and creating
- Emotional intelligence
- Problem solving
- Applying intuition

It is also worth considering any new skills you would love to learn or areas you would love to gain experience in. Would your ideal role give you the opportunity to learn new things on the job or enable you to study for a new skill you've been wanting to learn?

2. What types of people do you want to work with or serve?

Most jobs include interactions with other people in the form of those you work *with* (colleagues, managers, partners) and those whom you *serve* (customers, clients, students, patients, the general public or other living beings such as animals or things from the natural world). There is quite often a clear connection between those or that which you choose to serve and your purpose or calling.

Imagining your ideal role and the groups of people (or things) you would love to *serve*:

- Who are you drawn to helping in connection with you living out your purpose and calling? For example, young adults struggling with their mental health.

- What motivate you to want to do your job? For example, abandoned animals or endangered species.

- Which groups of people do you feel you can add most value to the lives of? For example, women business owners.

Thinking about those you would love to work *with*:

- What types of people bring out the best in you? For example, supportive, intelligent, ambitious people.

- What types of people motivate you to go to work? For example, fun, upbeat, creative, inspiring, collaborative people.

- From past experience, what types of people would you rather *not* work with? For example, competitive, negative, narrow-minded people.

3. *What level of responsibility are you looking for?*

Are you looking to take a step up through your next role? Does alignment for you mean having more impact at a higher level? Are you considering going into a role at entry level in order to learn the ropes first? What level do you feel would enable a life of greater balance?

Here are some of the different levels of responsibility:

- Owner
- Senior manager
- Chief executive officer
- Middle manager
- Director
- Manager
- Partner
- Team member/associate

Consider whether a step up the ladder is something that you truly want for yourself or whether you are wanting it because of an external expectation that that is what you 'should' do next.

4. What salary and benefits are you looking for?

What is the ideal salary you would love to be earning each month or each year? And what other benefits would you love to receive as part of your remuneration package?

For example:

- Private medical insurance
- Pension
- Wellness programmes
- Gym membership
- Car allowance
- Childcare vouchers
- Holidays
- Staff discounts

I recommend that you aim high here and also consider the bottom line remuneration package you would accept if you found the job of your dreams. If you don't already have one, it can be helpful to create a survival budget so that you know what you are able to accept as your minimum salary to cover your bills and perhaps an aspect of your lifestyle.

5. What type of working environment would you thrive in?

It is also worth considering the type of working environment which would be the best fit for you as this can impact your mood, your wellbeing and your effectiveness.

Do you prefer to be more active and on your feet or relatively static in front of a computer? Do you find it more stimulating to be around lots of other people and perhaps members of the public in a more sociable working space? Maybe you prefer the solitude of remote working or being out in nature? Or maybe a hybrid of the two to create some balance?

Here are a few different types of environment for you to consider:

- Traditional/office
- Sociable/public-facing
- Creative/stimulating
- Outdoors/natural
- Remote/solitary
- Hybrid

The employer

Let's now consider what type of employer might be the best fit for you. You may have some strong feelings about this based on your past experiences or you may feel very open to aligning with your purpose through a number of different types of employer.

Here are some questions to ask yourself to gain clarity on your aligned employer.

1. What is the purpose of your aligned employer?

The best starting point for narrowing down a potential employer who might align with *your* purpose, is simply to focus in on *their* purpose. Here are some organisations and their purpose to help illustrate this point:

- **The Open University** – To promote educational opportunity and social justice

- **Age UK** – To support older people in need

- **Bupa** – To help people live longer, healthier and happier lives

- **Patagonia** – To save our home planet

- **TOMS** – To use business to improve people's lives

How important is it for you to work for an organisation with a strong sense of purpose? How important is it that this matches with your own purpose? Would you be happy to work for an organisation which enables you to have your ideal role, but which puts profit before people? Or do you want to work for one which has a social mission or an underlying cause which they are championing?

The concept of the 'purpose-led' organisation has gained much momentum over recent years and presents more choices for workers now looking to find an employer who might share some of the same values.

What might the purpose of your aligned employer be?

2. What size of organisation might allow you to align most with your values?

The size of an organisation is a factor which can directly impact your values. For instance, working in a corporate environment can present more opportunities to align with the values of growth, social interaction and diversity. Alternatively, a smaller company might have more of a family feel and enable you to make a bigger impact or feel the excitement of watching it grow.

Here are the different sizes of organisation to consider:

- **Micro** – under ten people

- **SME** – under 250 people

- **Large organisation** – over 250 people

- **Global organisation** – operating in a number of countries

What size of employer do you feel would enable you to align most with your values?

3. How important is the location of your employer?

With the advent of remote working, employer location has become less of a consideration over recent years, but it is still one worth questioning. Perhaps you have realised how important human connection is to you and therefore prefer to work in an office with others? Or how much you appreciate the separation of your work and home life?

If you are looking at a new role which cannot be done remotely, then you will need to consider how much of a commute you are prepared to have. Some people enjoy time on the train, for instance, where they can listen to a podcast or prepare for the day ahead. Others find it a drain on their energy.

Maybe you prefer a city location so you can socialise after work, or somewhere more local where you can perhaps walk or cycle to work with green space nearby? Or maybe you are considering a house move and therefore focused on a certain location?

How important is it for you to work in physical proximity to other people?

What distance from your home are you prepared to travel?

Where would your aligned employer ideally be located?

4. *What type of work culture aligns with your values?*

The culture of an organisation is much harder to define than its purpose, however it is still an important aspect to consider as it can have a significant impact on your happiness at work. Culture encompasses the values, beliefs, behaviours and customs which can be seen and felt through the inner workings of an organisation as well as their dealings with the outer world.

There is both a written and unwritten aspect to culture which often only emerges when you are immersed in it for some time. However, you can set your *intention* here for what your aligned work culture is. This might be based on past experience of the type of culture which you thrived in or, conversely, the type of culture where you felt crushed and would not choose to work in again.

What type of culture have you tended to fit well into in any of your roles? What type of culture has felt out of alignment with who you are?

Here are some ideas on the different types of culture to spark your thinking:

- Results-orientated
- Collaborative
- Creative
- Supportive
- Flexible
- Hierarchical
- Family
- Competitive

- Forward-thinking
- Dynamic
- Innovative
- Entrepreneurial
- Nurturing
- Energetic
- People-focused
- Transparent

5. What wellbeing-related policies or benefits are important to you?

Here are some of the things you might choose to look out for in a new employer which could have a direct impact on your balance and wellbeing:

- **Working hours** – is it important to you to find an employer with flexible hours so you can manage your other priorities or maybe to be able to work part-time? Or are you happy to work full-time, so long as you can leave at a set time and work in a culture where this is not frowned upon?

- **Wellbeing-related benefits** – does your aligned employer provide benefits such as gym membership, lunchtime yoga, unlimited holidays or social activities which could positively impact your wellbeing?

- **Wellbeing policies** – does your aligned employer have a clear workplace wellbeing policy in place or a policy which can protect your mental health? Maybe a policy relating to parental leave or childcare is important to you.

You might also find it helpful to reflect on what you appreciate about your current or most recent employer and that you would look for in a new one.

Self-employment

Of course, traditional employment is not for everyone. You may have come to the realisation at this point, that you are not going to find what you are looking for by working for someone else and that the best fit for you is to work for yourself. There are more opportunities than ever to do the work you love through self-employment.

The main types of self-employment to consider are:

- **Freelancing/consulting** – working for a number of different clients on a flexible basis.

- **Contracting** – typically working for one client for a fixed period of time.

- **Sole trader** – a business which one person owns and manages.

- **Partnership** – a business set up and managed with at least one other person.

- **Limited company** – a business where you can employ others and have shareholders.

Each has its benefits and drawbacks and it could be that you choose one of these options for now in order to dip your toe in the water. For example, you may decide that freelancing or consulting is the easiest way forward but that longer term you aspire to set up your own limited company where you can build a team.

There are more details on how to begin setting up in business in the UK on the following Government website https://www.gov.uk/set-up-business.

The benefits of working for yourself

Working for yourself can be massively rewarding and offers many benefits versus regular employment. There is now a huge amount of resource and support available to enable people to become self-employed and it could be a great fit for you, especially if you are ready for a fresh challenge or have had an strong urge to follow this route.

Some of the many benefits to working for yourself which may align with your values include:

- Freedom
- Flexibility
- Challenge
- Autonomy

- Personal growth
- Creativity
- Purpose
- Making an impact

Is self-employment for you?

I have come to realise through my client work that self-employment is definitely not for everyone. If you are considering it, I recommend going into it with your eyes wide open and not as a knee-jerk reaction to how you feel about your current or most recent employer. Be really honest with yourself about your motivations.

The reality of self-employment is that:

- You may be working on your own for long periods.

- Your income might not be as regular or predictable.

- You may need to put yourself out there in order to generate interest or business.

- You may also need to wear many hats within your business beyond what you originally sign up for, for example, marketeer, accountant, salesperson.

For some this can be an exciting challenge and for others it can be a reason not to go into self-employment. Some of these realities can be worked around or may just be temporary as you get established. For example, over time you may bring other people into your business to support you. Or you may get a regular income stream from an ongoing client or product sale.

Qualities needed for self-employment

Having been self-employed for some time and having studied those who have become successful in self-employment, there are a number of personal qualities which stand out as being important. If you are considering this option yourself, I believe that you need to be:

- Resilient
- Motivated
- Disciplined
- Organised
- Courageous

- Patient
- Adaptable
- Driven
- Confident
- Independent

How many of these did you identify when you took the inventory on your personal qualities? Don't worry if you don't identify with all of them, as you can also see self-employment as an opportunity to develop some new strengths. The most crucial thing is to take an honest look within from the start as to whether this is a good fit for you. And, if so, to then just go for it!

Limiting belief check-in

If you have been considering working for yourself for some time, but have fears and doubts about it which have been holding you back, make a note of them now in your journal. Call out any limiting beliefs and take them through the exercise in Chapter 4. It is very normal for these types of thoughts and feelings to arise and not a sign that you shouldn't take this step.

Shortlisting and assessing your options

I recommend you take some time over the next week or two to reflect on this chapter, do some research and come up with a shortlist of upto six potential career options. They could be from a mix of different sectors or employers or from within your current employer and could include self-employment. You can also list your current role, if it is still a contender.

Once you have your shortlist of options, it is important that you then sense check how much they are aligned with the four roots of your Purpose Tree.

Download your free Career Path Assessment Worksheet in the Book Resources, which you can access through this link:

rebeccakirk.co.uk/book-resources

Which option comes through with the highest score? You can now enter that option into your Purpose Tree worksheet.

If you still don't have clarity

If at this stage you are still feeling a little lost and unsure, please don't despair. The timing of everyone's path is unique and it can't be rushed. If you have made it through the preceding chapters of this book and put some time and thought into the exercises, then you have already made a massive step forward.

This process is a *journey*. Check any feelings of doubt or dismay if you don't have total clarity on what's next for you just yet. Stay open to any thoughts and ideas over the coming weeks. Keep your energy light. Let go of any grasping. Trust in the groundwork you have done to guide you.

Remember your Higher Purpose and your Life Purpose – both of which can be accessed here and now. You can still make an impact and live out your purpose in what you are doing currently. How you do your job is in many ways as important as what you do. See the opportunity to make more impact now whilst you figure out the details of an alternative path. Or even if you don't have a job right now, in your interactions with others and through prayer or transmitting positive energy.

CHAPTER HIGHLIGHTS

- Drawing the four roots of your Purpose Tree together enables you to make the connections to identify your aligned career path options.

- Stating your prosperity goal will serve as a motivating force for moving you into action.

- Any new career ideas must be sense-checked against the four roots of your Purpose Tree to assess the level of alignment.

- If you don't have full clarity yet, remember this is a journey and to stay light and open to possibilities and to trust your own path.

Whatever you can do, or dream you can, begin it. Boldness has genius, power and magic in it.

GOETHE

CHAPTER 14:
Your Career Alignment Plan

If you're tired of feeling unfulfilled and you know now more than ever that it's time to transform your working life, then all the insights and discoveries you have made from reading this book must lead to committed action. This final chapter is where we draw upon the concepts, practices and ideas which have emerged and turn them into actionable route map which leads you to your purpose and to a place where greater happiness and fulfilment reside.

Wherever you are currently at on your Career Alignment Journey, this chapter will bring you the necessary focus to begin taking immediate steps towards your career transformation so that you can start living the more purposeful life you signed up for. That focus comes in the form of a Career Alignment Plan.

Your Career Alignment Plan is a one-page summary of the why, the what, the how and the when of your transformation. It consists of three parts:

- An intention
- Inspired actions
- A set of goals

Download your free Career Alignment Plan Worksheet in the Book Resources which you can access through this link:

rebeccakirk.co.uk/book-resources

1. Intention

I have always been a fan of setting goals and giving myself something tangible to aim for. But I also know that goals can sometimes fall short when used in isolation. Recently, after years of setting myself a particular financial business goal, I decided to take a different tack. There was something about this goal which seemed to keep me in a state of grasping. The energy behind it felt as if it belonged more in the corporate world I had emerged from and not the world I now inhabited. I resisted it.

When I reflect on my days as a business owner, and perhaps even before then, I realise that I have never been able to fully connect with a purely monetary goal. There has always been something missing for me. I think I have had a sense that there will only be a temporary satisfaction to reaching such a goal. And that, as was my experience in the corporate world, once I have achieved it, there will be a new and bigger financial goal to take its place. I needed something deeper and more lasting.

During a recent trip to India, I had the head space and heart space to really focus on my intention for the year ahead. And, in essence, it all boiled down to this: fulfilling my purpose and my potential. This is what truly mattered to me. I could feel it in my bones. And so, I set this as my intention, not only for the year ahead, but until I no longer felt it in my bones.

Setting the intention to fulfil my purpose and potential created a powerful ripple effect across the whole of my working life. I felt much more relaxed within my work and my client interactions and spent more of my energy on supporting them and less on how or whether I was going to meet my financial goal. The difference was noticeable. And the irony was that more money started to flow anyway. My higher vibration made me a match to those people and opportunities which helped me attract more prosperity on the way to realising my intention.

What makes an intention different to a goal

Your plan involves setting both intentions *and* goals as there is a different energy behind each one and the two combined create a powerful synergy to propel you forward, whilst also enabling you to enjoy the journey more.

An intention is simply something which you wish to bring about. It might seem at first glance very similar to a goal, however, what makes an intention special and different to a goal is that it:

- Is heart-based rather than head-based which leads to greater fulfilment.

- Focuses you on the journey as well as the destination.

- Provides you with an overall direction of travel to guide you every day.

- Puts you into a positive, high vibration state which will help you attract the right people and circumstances.

- Is flexible and allows for any unforeseen life happenings.

- Brings a sense of expansion and a means of seeing the bigger picture.

- Enables a deeper, more empowered connection to your goals and actions.

- Relates to your 'being' state and how you want to feel as opposed to just your 'doing' or 'having' state.

- Opens you up to greater abundance than you might experience just with a goal.

- Leads to less grasping and thereby greater inner peace and calm.

Declaring your intention

So hopefully you can see that it is well worth the time and effort to set an intention before you set your goals. Now, let's look at clarifying what *your* intention is. It may well be that you already have a clear sense of this from working through this book. Perhaps something has emerged for you and your Higher Self is already whispering the answer. But if you aren't clear yet, then the suggestions below could spark something for you.

Here are some ideas of intentions which might link in with your **Career Purpose**:

- My intention is to feel fulfilled and joyful in my working life.

- My intention is to live out my calling.

- My intention is to realise my true potential.

- My intention is to express my creativity through my work.

- My intention is to make a bigger impact in the world.

- My intention is to share my gifts and talents with the world.

You may instead feel more drawn to choosing an intention which brings greater connection to your **Life Purpose** such as:

- My intention is to live out my purpose every day.

- My intention is to spread love and light on the planet.

- My intention is to be of service to others.

Or perhaps your **Higher Purpose**:

- My intention is to awaken to my Higher Purpose.

- My intention is to live in connection with my Higher Self.

- My intention is to grow and evolve as a spiritual being.

Which one of those resonates with you most? Ultimately, I refer you to your own inner guidance and to articulate your intention in a way which you feel most connected to deep within. You may need a little time to reflect on this. If you feel you are struggling to decide what it is, I recommend that you take time out and go for a walk in nature or spend time meditating and asking your Higher Self to guide you.

2. Goals

To bring your intention to life and gain further focus and direction, I now recommend creating a set of goals which sit underneath your intention. Your goals will be different to your intention in that they will have a very *specific* and *measurable* outcome.

The benefits of a well-set goal are that it will:

- Provide you with a powerful focus.

- Help you channel your time, energy and resources.

- Enable you to create a motivating vision of your future.

- Ground your intention.

Motivation is key in ensuring that you convert your goals into action. This is where I recommend you refer back to your values. Your values are a source of deep motivation for you. When my clients have set goals which honour their values, there has been an innate driving force behind them which has meant that they have gone on to achieve what they set out to. For example, goals which have taken them towards greater freedom, greater creativity or greater peace have proved highly motivating.

Staging your goals

Timing is another crucial element in setting an effective goal. Without a timescale for your goal, you are more likely to let it drift. So, I encourage you to spend some time considering *when* you want it to happen. This is, of course, dependant on the action steps you need to take and what is achievable in the time you have available.

Equally, setting a goal with an unrealistic time frame, whilst perhaps demonstrating your eagerness, can also lead to demotivation if you don't achieve it which can stop you from making any further progress.

In the Career Alignment Plan worksheet, you will see a space for short-, medium- and long-term goals. As a guide, this is how that could translate into more specific time frames for you:

- Short term: the goals you plan to make happen in the next **three months**

- Medium term: the goals you plan to make happen in the next **six to twelve months**

- Long term: the goals you plan to make happen in the next **two to three years**

I recommend that, where possible, you commit to a *specific* date for each goal, particularly for your short-term goals. You can then revisit your plan as it evolves and add some specific dates in for your medium- and long-term goals.

You may find it helpful to consider the time frame aspect of your goals *after* you have listed out the actions in your plan so you can take into account time-critical elements such as the notice period of your current job or the length of a course of study.

Staging your goals can also help reduce the debilitating effects of overwhelm. This is particularly significant if you are considering making a complete career change. Overwhelm is a very common experience once you've decided on what you want to do. Planning out your next steps in a way which considers any financial or time constraints means that you can transition into your new career over time. This creates breathing space and a higher vibration.

If you are looking to take the Stepping Stone Pathway, staging your goals can assist in maintaining your motivation. Whilst your immediate reality may not be exactly what you want, having longer term goals helps you to keep one eye on your ultimate desire. It's a way of 'putting it out there' to the Universe and committing to your destination.

Clarifying your goals

We will now explore some ideas for your goals and how they can help you manifest your intention. These will be presented in relation to the three different Career Alignment Pathways so that you can draw on the ideas and practices from previous chapters. You may also have your own ideas for goals or find it helpful to refer to your journal notes on other things which have resonated with you.

Whatever your goals are, if you want to make them effective it is important that they are *specific* and something which you can *measure*. In the sample Career Alignment Plans I share with you later in this chapter, you can see what a specific and measurable goal looks like, and how your intention, goals and inspired actions can work together as a whole.

Suggested goals: The Realigned Pathway

For guidance on potential goals within this pathway, we will refer back to the ways in which you can realign within your current role which we looked at in Chapter 12: purpose, values, gifts, balance, confidence and acceptance. Even if you are going down one of the other pathways, you may still choose to set one of these as a short-term goal to make your current situation more liveable. As you look through the suggested goals, consider how you might measure each one.

Purpose goals

- To reconnect with your employer's vision and mission

- To spread more kindness and compassion in your day-to-day interactions

- To begin volunteering at a local animal shelter one day per week

- To have a daily meditation practice which connects you to your Higher Purpose

Values goals

- To create more **autonomy** within your current role

- To have weekly **support** meetings with your manager

- To set aside one evening every week for your **creative** pursuits

- To build **human connection** by spending more time in the office

Gifts and goals

- To begin a training course to gain a new skill or strength

- To have a mentor to help you develop your leadership skills

- To delegate certain tasks to allow you to focus on your skills and strengths

Balance goals

- To create a stronger boundary between work and home

- To set up a separate office space

- To attend a weekly yoga class

- To immerse yourself in nature every day

Confidence goals

- To enjoy regularly contributing in team meetings

- To feel more at ease talking about your gifts

- To put yourself forward for a work project or promotion

- To show up at work more authentically

Acceptance goals

- To feel at peace with the choices you have made and your career history

- To accept the people who you work with just as they are
- To practice acceptance around the financial need to stay in your current job in the short term

Suggested goals: The New Pathway

If you have decided to make a complete career change and you are ready to get started, then here are some of the types of goals you might consider.

If your aim is to be working in a new role in a new sector which aligns with your purpose, then your goals might be:

- To hand in your notice on your current job
- To leave your current job (by a certain date)
- To become qualified in a new field
- To establish connections with people in the new sector
- To gain experience in the new sector

In your plan, be specific with the name of the job, the employer and the sector if you know that detail now.

If your career change involves working for yourself, then you may set such goals as:

- Registering your business
- Launching your new website
- Launching your first product
- Welcoming your first paying customer
- Having a certain number of customers

- Reaching a certain income

- Attracting a particular customer or client

Suggested goals: The Stepping Stone Pathway

If you are taking the Stepping Stone Pathway then here are some examples of the types of short- or medium-term goals you might choose to set:

- To move into a similar job within a new sector which connects you with your preferred area of calling

- To start a new job with your current employer which aligns more with your purpose

- To move into a similar job for a new employer which is more aligned with your values

- To become a freelancer within your current line of work

As we saw in Chapter 12, your next step could be about exploring something new alongside your current role. If you are considering this, then you might choose to set one of these types of goals:

- To reduce to part-time hours

- To begin volunteering one day per week

- To set aside a certain amount of time each week for your creative pursuits

- To save up a certain amount of money to enable you to retrain

- To spend certain days each week focusing on turning your hobby into a business

- To earn a certain amount of money each month from your side business, so that you can leave your main job

You can then consider what your longer-term goal is, such as:

- To set up your own business in a new sector
- To begin working full-time in a brand new career

Goals to set if you still need further clarity

Even if you aren't sure yet which pathway to take or what your purpose is, you can still set some goals. In fact, I highly recommend that you do, so that you are still able to work towards your intention and maintain motivation. It will also enable you to put a time limit around any period of reflection or a career break.

Here are some examples of the types of goals you might want to set:

- To have clarity on which career pathway to choose
- To maintain a Daily Spiritual Practice which enables you to receive guidance and clarity on your career path
- To connect with your Life Purpose through your daily interactions
- To raise your vibration so that you can be a match for your aligned career path
- To begin exploring a new passion or hobby which could become a new career path

Use positive language

As with your intention, make sure that when setting your goals, you use language which is positive and motivating. So, for example, rather than saying "I will leave this job that I hate", you would articulate it along the lines of "I will move into a fulfilling new job". I always say to my clients that the true test of a goal is how motivated and excited you feel by it and language plays a big part in that. It's about *feeling* what the right goal is and not just *thinking*.

3. Inspired actions

The final aspect of your Career Alignment Plan is to consider the actions you feel inspired to take to achieve your goal and your intention. These inspired actions might be practical steps such as researching a new role or they could be of a more spiritual nature such as meditation, prayer, or visualisation. Be sure not to confuse your inspired actions with your goals. Your goals are typically bigger and more motivating. The actions are the individual steps that are going to help you achieve your goal.

Listing out your inspired actions will enable you to:

- Ground your intention.

- Reduce any overwhelm by breaking down your goals into smaller steps.

- Sense check the timings of your goals, by considering what it actually involves to achieve them.

- Bring further focus and clarity to your Career Alignment Plan.

I recommend you list out at least *three* inspired actions to take towards each of your goals in your Career Alignment Plan.

Look at each of your goals and ask yourself questions such as:

- What am I feeling drawn to doing right now to make that goal a reality?

- What is the simplest of next steps I could take which will move me forward?

- Where am I being called to go, who am I being called to speak to?

Consciously connect with your intuition, both whilst doing this exercise and in the days or weeks after to see what emerges. Even if the action doesn't make total sense to you, follow the trail. You never know what or who it might lead you to.

Sample Career Alignment Plans

On the following pages are four samples of Career Alignment Plans which focus in on the intention 'To feel fulfilled and joyful in my working life' and illustrate how this might be achieved via the different Career Alignment Pathways. Plus, there is a sample of a plan which can be used for anyone who is still not clear on which pathway to take.

Sample Career Alignment Plan 1:
The Realigned Pathway

Intention		
To feel fulfilled and joyful in my working life		
Short-term goal	**Medium-term goal**	**Long-term goal**
To live out my Life Purpose by being of service to others and sharing my light every day.	To join a local animal charity and spend at least one hour per week volunteering.	To be a more confident and effective leader in my current role.
Timeframe	**Timeframe**	**Timeframe**
Within next 7 days	Within next 3 months	Within next 12 months
Inspired actions	**Inspired actions**	**Inspired actions**
1. Smile at the people I pass on my morning walk 2. Feed the birds on my garden each morning 3. Offer a listening ear to my friend who is going through a difficult time	1. Research local animal charities and apply to join 2. Reduce time spent on social media by one hour each week to create time for volunteering 3. Block out time in my calendar	1. Speak to my boss about options to develop my leadership skills 2. Do some leadership training 3. Find a mentor at work to support me in building confidence and becoming a better leader

Sample Career Alignment Plan 2:
The New Pathway

Intention		
To feel fulfilled and joyful in my working life		
Short-term goal	**Medium-term goal**	**Long-term goal**
To begin a training course to become a coach.	To qualify as a coach and set up my own coaching business.	To be working with at least 5 clients at any one time.
Timeframe	**Timeframe**	**Timeframe**
Within next 6 weeks	Within next 12 months	Within next 18 months
Inspired actions	**Inspired actions**	**Inspired actions**
1. Check my finances to see how much I can afford to invest into a course 2. Research the best fit course 3. Set up a comfortable and inspiring space to study	1. Make a study schedule to keep me on track 2. Set out my initial coaching package/ offer for clients 3. Create a website and register business with Google	1. List my services on coaching directories 2. Write 3 blog articles which will attract my ideal clients 3. Set up a mailing list and create a free resource for signing up

Sample Career Alignment Plan 3:
The Stepping Stone Pathway

Intention		
To feel fulfilled and joyful in my working life		
Short-term goal	**Medium-term goal**	**Long-term goal**
To spend one evening each week exploring my creative passion for garden design.	To begin my first (pro bono) garden design project.	To be working full time as a garden designer.
Timeframe	**Timeframe**	**Timeframe**
Within next 2 weeks	Within next 6 months	Within next 2 years
Inspired actions	**Inspired actions**	**Inspired actions**
1. Put a designated evening aside in my calendar each week and commit to finishing work on time that day 2. Read about the journeys of other garden designers 3. Research what qualifications are needed and what courses of study are available	1. Begin an online course in garden design which I can do one evening each week 2. Ask colleagues, friends and family if they would like some help redesigning their garden 3. Delegate some of my existing weekend responsibilities to free up time to work on the project	1. Create a vision board of my new working life 2. Visit an award-winning garden each month to stay inspired 3. Make a financial plan to be able to leave my current job

Sample Career Alignment Plan 4:
If you need further clarity

Intention		
To feel fulfilled and joyful in my working life		
Short-term goal	**Medium-term goal**	**Long-term goal**
To create space for clarity and guidance with a 10 minute Daily Spiritual Practice of meditation and Higher Self intuitive writing.	To spend at least one evening a week pursuing a new or existing passion/hobby.	To have clarity around the new career path I want to pursue.
Timeframe	**Timeframe**	**Timeframe**
Within next 7 days	Within next 4 weeks	Within next 6 months
Inspired actions	**Inspired actions**	**Inspired actions**
1. Clear out the spare room and create a small altar where I can do my practice 2. Buy a beautiful new journal for my intuitive writing practice 3. Set my alarm 10 minutes earlier each day	1. Give myself permission to do more of the things I enjoy (cooking, reading) 2. Research local classes and workshops and sign up for one 3. Put a new boundary in place to protect this time	1. Create a survival budget to give me breathing space to do some further reflection 2. Practice manifestation of my intention each day 3. Stay aware of any signs or intuitive feelings and start to act on them

Elevate your Career Alignment Plan to a higher dimension

As we approach the end of the book, I want to leave you with a sprinkle of inspiration with which to elevate your Career Alignment Plan to a higher dimension. These spiritual practices will infuse your plan and your onward journey with a powerful energy and put you in the best position to make your intention and your goals a reality. They will also allow you to enjoy the journey more and to stay calm and peaceful as your plan evolves.

Manifestation

Manifestation is the act of attracting something you want into your life as a result of your thoughts and your vibration. Manifestation works once you have *clarity* on what it is you want to bring into being. You might choose to focus on manifesting your intention or your individual goals.

Manifestation transforms your Career Alignment Plan from something static into something dynamic. It opens up a powerful energy stream and a connection with the higher realms. By practising manifestation, you will feel more empowered, like you are a co-creator in your reality. Also, when you manifest, as you are focused on what you *do* want, it naturally stops you from focusing on your current situation and what you *don't* want.

There are many ways in which you can use manifestation to bring your Career Alignment Plan into being. Essentially, they all point towards raising your vibration and enabling you to come into resonance with the vibration of that which you want. You may also apply some of the suggestions from Chapter 2, such as getting out into nature, working with a crystal or an essential oil to add to your manifestation practice.

Here are three simple steps to get you started in becoming a powerful manifestor:

1. Check in on your thoughts and beliefs

The first step is to become very conscious of any thoughts or beliefs you have in connection with what you want to manifest. As we know, thoughts hold a vibration so it's important to check in on whether they are supportive of your intention and goals.

If you find that you have any resistance or limiting beliefs in connection with your Career Alignment Plan and what you want to manifest, then revisit the exercise for releasing those beliefs in Chapter 4.

2. Visualise

Visualisation is a proven technique for reaching goals and outcomes through mental visual imagery. It can be used to bring your Career Alignment Plan to life and give it more colour, more emotion and more clarity. You can do this by simply using your imagination or you can do something more tangible by creating a vision board.

A vision board is a collage of images and words which represent what you want to achieve. It can be powerfully motivating to look at your vision board each day, connecting you with the positive emotion which it triggers and keeping you focused and on track. You might choose to include a phrase, such as your intention or an affirmation. Or perhaps a photo of yourself of when you previously felt empowered, happy or fulfilled.

The most important element of visualisation is to connect with the *emotion* behind what you want to have happen. What does it actually *feel* like when you imagine having what you want?

This allows you to get into alignment with the vibration which will resonate with what you want so that it can come into your experience.

Here is a suggestion of some of the types of things you might visualise in connection with your Career Alignment Plan:

- Happily chatting with your friends about your fulfilling new job

- Buzzing as you enter your new workspace and meet your new colleagues

- Feeling purposeful and content giving your time to help others as a volunteer

- A wave of happiness and excitement on a Sunday evening as you contemplate the week ahead

- Having fun with a creative activity at the weekend such as cooking, drawing or crafting

- Excitedly running your own business, interacting with clients

- A sense of calm as you go about your day after your Daily Spiritual Practice

3. Release your desire

The next step is to simply release your desire out to the Universe. Here are some steps I invite you to follow so that you can get the most value from it:

- **Say it out loud**. Verbalise the intention or goal you want to manifest three times.

- **Meditate on it.** Spend a few minutes connecting with it from your heart centre and tuning into the energy behind it and how it makes you feel.

- **Release it.** Imagine that you are sending your intention out into the Universe, as if you were releasing a bird or a balloon.

- **Let go of the outcome**. Drop any grasping or expectation for your intention to happen right away.

- **Open up to receive**. Become aware and receptive to what comes your way, trusting it will be for your highest good.

Bring this into your Daily Spiritual Practice so that you can feel it and live it each day.

Faith

Faith can move mountains. I truly believe that. And it is also one of your greatest allies on your Career Alignment Journey, whatever stage you are at right now. Faith in this context is about having total trust in the Universe and an unerring belief in that which you cannot as yet see or touch. And it's about knowing that you are being guided and supported by a higher force.

With faith, you are able to:

- *Move with* the flow instead of against it.

- Accept your current situation knowing that all things are changing and that challenges are part of our human experience.

- Let go of grasping and chasing and trying to control every detail and instead offer your desires to the Universe.

- Stay present whilst your plan and your vision are being worked on in the background.

- Connect to the Source of everything, whether that is new people, new income streams or new opportunities.

And with all of this inevitably comes a higher vibration which resonates with what you are wishing to manifest on your plan.

Conversely, without faith, if things don't immediately fall into place, it is easy to slip into a state of despondency, or to give up whenever any obstacles appear. This will lower your vibration so that you continue to match the circumstances that you *don't* want. I encourage you to stay conscious of your overriding emotions and energetic state, if and when any challenges appear along your path.

My Mum used to have a saying which always helped me through times when things weren't quite happening on my preferred timescales or in the way I had hoped, "God moves in mysterious ways". Sometimes, we cannot see the full picture and it might seem like things are working against us. But often things are being manoeuvred in a way which is beyond our mind's comprehension.

As we explored in Chapter 1, understanding Divine Timing can be a game-changer when it comes to navigating your path. Your Ego Self might be getting frustrated that things aren't changing for you as quickly as you want. However, your Higher Self knows that there is a divine plan which is unfolding for you. And that this is a perfectly timed change which may bring with it certain tests and lessons which will serve to make you stronger in the long run. Perhaps there is more for you to learn in your current job before moving on. Your Higher Self knows that sometimes we are subject to a holding pattern whilst things are being lined up for us in the background.

Stay tuned in

After you have done your manifestation practice and connected with faith, I recommend that you then tune into any guidance and opportunities which get presented to you. You might consider this guidance coming directly from the Universe itself or perhaps from your spirit guide.

The guidance can come in the form of:

- Serendipitous happenings, such as a chance meeting with a future boss.

- A message sent through your dreams.

- Recurring symbols or signs with a message behind them, such as number patterns, animals or insects.

- Intuitive ideas and feelings.

Remember that your intuition is your inbuilt guidance system which passes messages on to you and is a vital tool for helping you manifest your plan. For example, I have had clients who received intuitive nudges out of the blue such as an urge to visit a local shop which then led to their artwork being displayed and sold which kick-started their business. Or an urge to get back in touch with an old colleague which led them towards a role in a new sector.

Sophia's story

Sophia came to me a few years ago desperately unhappy in her job and her marriage on the verge of breaking down. She was struggling to see a way out of her situation and longed for guidance and direction on where to take her career and how to achieve a better working life which aligned with her values.

Over the course of several sessions, we worked towards creating her Career Alignment Plan. Her intention was to 'align with her true purpose' and one of her main goals was to set up her own architecture business which afforded her greater work life balance.

Sophia began to unpick the resistance and blocks which had been getting in the way of making a break for it and started shifting her negative thought patterns. She began a Daily Spiritual Practice of meditation, gratitude, visualisation and intention setting which elevated her vibration and helped her become a powerful magnet for what she wanted.

Just two months later, I received an email from her which read, "I've had a crazy week! So, the architecture business which I've started has really taken off! I went out to two enquiries last week. One of which has expressed a wish to employ me and agreed to a massive fee that I still can't believe! Another one is waiting for a fee proposal and seems keen. Plus, I met with the head of undergraduate architecture at my local university today and she's more or less assured me that I have secured a post to teach first year in September for one day a week to start with. I'm so happy!"

A prayer for your onward journey

Dear Universe,

I offer my plan up to you, trusting that you know the best way for it to unfold. Let me get out of my own way so that I may rest easy in this knowledge.

Please grant me the courage to face the things which scare me but which bring me into closer alignment with my purpose. And the patience and faith to work to your timing instead of my own.

If there is anything left for me to learn from my current situation, I pray for the grace with which to accept it. And to choose to see any obstacles as opportunities to help me evolve on my spiritual path instead of reasons that my plan won't come to fruition.

I vow to listen to the guidance you offer me and to my own inner voice which is lovingly moving me towards the realisation of my plan. Safe in the knowledge that you have already handled the details and that my true purpose already exists.

I release that which no longer serves me. And I open up to that which wants to enter.

I am ready.

CHAPTER HIGHLIGHTS

- An intention is your overarching 'why' and is more heart-based and generalised than your goals.

- Linking your goals with your values will create a deeper motivation.

- Staging your goals (into short-, medium- and long-term) will also keep you motivated and reduce feelings of overwhelm.

- You can practice manifesting your Career Alignment Plan by checking in on your thoughts and beliefs, releasing your intention and visualising your goals.

- Faith is one of your greatest allies on your Career Alignment Journey.

- Pay attention to any guidance given in the form of dreams, serendipitous events, recurring signs and intuitive feelings.

References

Chapter 1
1. Thubten, G. (2019). A Monk's Guide to Happiness: Meditation in the 21st century. Yellow Kite.

Chapter 2
2. Hawkins, D. (2020). *The Map of Consciousness Explained:* A Proven Energy Scale to Actualize Your Ultimate Potential. Hay House UK.

3. Hole, J., Hirsch, M., Ball, E., Meads, C. (2015). Music as an aid for postoperative recovery in adults: a systematic review and meta-analysis. The Lancet, volume 386, issue 10004.

4. Tolle, E. (2018). A New Earth. Penguin Random House.

Chapter 3
5. Kondo, M. (2014). The Life Changing Magic of Tidying. Vermillion.

6. Silver, T. (2019). It's Not Your Money: How to Live Fully from Divine Abundance. Hay House, pp.38

Chapter 5
7. www.urbandictionary.com/define.php?term=Awakened

8. Bridges, W. (2004). Transitions: Making Sense of Life's Changes. Da Capo Press.

9. Jeffers, S, "Bringing more love into the world", https://susanjeffers.com/2022/05/02/bringing-more-love-into-the-world/

10. Sinetar, M. (1987). Do What You Love, the Money Will Follow. Dell Publishing.

Chapter 8
11. https://dictionary.cambridge.org/dictionary/english/intuition

Take your search for purpose to the next level

The search for purpose and fulfilment can often be a lonely journey and it's all too easy to become discouraged or veer off course. If the ideas in this book have resonated with you and you're looking for some extra support and accountability to align with your purpose, then here are some of the ways in which we can connect more deeply.

One-to-one coaching. Personalised coaching sessions with me, fully focused on you and your career. My signature career coaching programme also includes workbooks and support with creating your own Daily Spiritual Practice. Accountability and encouragement come as standard!

Group coaching. Join a supportive community of other spiritually-minded people seeking purpose. Group programme includes live group coaching sessions with me, plus pre-recorded content and workbooks to deepen your journey. All with a focus on aligning with your purpose and making a conscious career change. (Launching soon – sign up to my newsletter for updates).

Resources. As well as regular content on my social media channels, you can also access some other free resources on my website. Including a career change quiz, an on demand career coaching webinar and spiritually-themed articles in my blog.

Newsletter. Join my mailing list and receive monthly ideas and inspirations designed to support you on your Career Alignment Journey. Featuring how-to articles, supportive practices, empowering quotes and personal stories.

Discover more at: rebeccakirk.co.uk

Acknowledgements

I am deeply grateful to so many people who have made this book possible in so many different ways. Here are just some of them.

Firstly, all of my wonderful clients for entrusting me as their coach. Without them this book would not have emerged. I honour you all for showing up, digging deep and doing the work.

Rob Bannister, my publisher for his infectious energy and his patience. He has generously shared his time and knowledge and made my book writing journey so much fun.

Ben Fletcher-Bates, the designer for his creativity, attention to detail and understanding in bringing my book vision to life.

Erin Chamberlain, my editor for encouraging me to write with confidence and for keeping my eye on the bigger picture.

Kathryn McCusker, my Kundalini Yoga teacher who inspired me to fall in love with this wonderful practice which transformed everything for me. Her energy and wisdom have helped keep me on track with my purpose through life's ups and downs.

Anna Melton, my friend and PR manager who gave me the kick I needed to 'come from behind the curtain' and start showing up as my true self in my work.

Helen Reuben, the coach who trained me to be a transpersonal coach in 2019 and who introduced me to A New Earth by Eckhart Tolle. Both changed my life.

Rebecca Campbell, Eckhart Tolle, Shakti Gawain, Tosha Silver, Richard Bolles, Wayne Dyer, Louise Hay and all the spiritual teachers whose wisdom has supported and inspired me and whose courage to tread the path before me has made my own journey more possible.

Sister Patricia Jordan for the example and inspiration of her unquestionable faith and joyful nature in service of others. Her friendship and spiritual guidance are a true blessing.

The amazing and talented women of Lucy Loveheart Creations who graciously supported me with my last career change and brought me some of my happiest working days.

All the people who have taken a chance on me over the course of my career, in particular, those who also turned out to be lifelong friends – Gabi Amato-Heape, Janice Robson and Debra Madden. And all the people who challenged me in my career for providing me with the catalyst for my awakening.

And last, but definitely not least, my family. Deep gratitude to Jo, my soulmate who has been by my side throughout this writing journey. Her patience, encouragement and calm nature have given me a steady anchor through the choppy waters of life. And her creativity and courage to put herself out there have been a constant source of inspiration to me.

My dear Dad for all of his advice, support and heartfelt interest in my work which I feel so blessed to have. The chats about my book on our many dog walks filled me with the encouragement, self-belief and joy to keep going. He has always been the wind beneath my wings.

Daniel, my brother who has been working as my unpaid coach and business guru since 2015. His entrepreneurial spirit and his infectious ability to think big and push the boundaries have helped me expand beyond all recognition.

Cassie, for generously welcoming me into her home in Sydney which made my life-changing career break possible and for providing me with a valuable sounding board for my spiritual side.

And finally, my Mum. She embodied so much of what this book is about and blazed a trail for me to follow. Without her example and her faith, this book would not have been written.

About the author

Rebecca began her career in the States as a retail buyer. She returned to the UK in 2001 and worked in the corporate world for Sainsbury's, Boots and other well-known brands, while often feeling like a round peg in a square hole.

In 2010 Rebecca embarked on a life-changing career break to Australia which led to a spiritual awakening and ultimately set her on the path to making her most profound career change, retraining as a life coach in 2016.

With Rebecca's unique approach to career coaching, she has enabled hundreds of clients from around the world to discover the clarity and confidence to navigate their career crossroads and awaken to a working life of greater purpose, peace and prosperity.

Rebecca has always called on her spirituality to support her in her own career. Her daily spiritual practices alongside her tried- and-tested coaching methods, allow her to gently guide others on their spiritual path whilst making breakthroughs in their career.

As a spiritual career coach, Rebecca now dedicates her work to following her calling to enable more people to awaken and live the life of purpose they were meant to live.